NEPAL

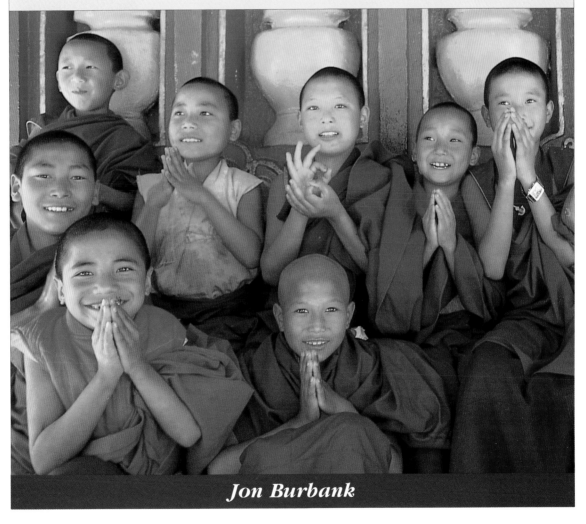

Jon Burbank

TIMES BOOKS INTERNATIONAL
Singapore • Kuala Lumpur

Cultures of the World

Editorial Director	Shirley Hew
Managing Editor	Shova Loh
Editors	Falaq Kagda
	Michael Spilling
	Sue Sismondo
	Roslind Varghese
	Azra Moiz
	Elizabeth Koh Kanematsu
	Jon Burbank
	Jim Goodman
Picture Editor	Yee May Kaung
Production	Anthoney Chua
Design	Tuck Loong
	Ronn Yeo
	Felicia Wong
	Loo Chuan Ming
Illustrator	Kelvin Sim
	Cherine Lim
	Andrew Chan
	Anuar bin Abdul Rahim

Originated and designed by
Times Books International,
an imprint of Times Editions Pte Ltd
Times Centre, 1 New Industrial Road
Singapore 536196
Tel: 2848844 Fax: 2854871

© Times Editions Pte Ltd 1991

Printed in Singapore by Welpac Printing & Packaging Pte Ltd

ISBN 981 204 282 2

INTRODUCTION

IF PEOPLE KNOW ABOUT NEPAL at all, they know it as the home of Mount Everest, the world's tallest mountain peak. The Himalayan mountains that stretch across Nepal's northern border contain eight of the 10 tallest mountains in the world. Nepal is also the birthplace of the Buddha and an important pilgrimage site for Hinduism.

Living on mountain sides and in narrow valleys are dozens of ethnic groups, speaking different languages and worshiping different gods. Somehow, all these groups have lived together in peace, even though Nepal is one of the poorest countries in the world.

This book acquaints us with a country that is not very well-known, but well worth learning about. It is one of the series, *Cultures of the World*, a look at people and their lifestyles around the world.

CONTENTS

This Tamang man comes from one of the many hill tribes in Nepal. The Tamangs often come down from their homes to the Kathmandu Valley in search of work.

CONTENTS

In the higher areas, a great deal of domestic life takes place on the rooftops of houses. It's the best place to dry crops and to bask in the warm sunshine.

GEOGRAPHY

MILLIONS OF YEARS AGO, the world was one big land mass called Gondwanaland. Gondwanaland came apart, and its pieces drifted over the ocean. As the years went by, the pieces of the land mass drifted further and further apart, and the waters that divided the land became today's oceans and seas. The land masses were broken up to form huge continents and tiny islands scattered all over the globe.

The story of Nepal began about 10–15 million years ago. Then, present-day India was separate from the continent of Asia. But earth movements pushed India closer and closer until finally it collided with Asia. The force that resulted from the meeting of two land masses pushed the land up, forming majestic mountains and hills. Thus Nepal was born.

Today, Nepal is a landlocked country, surrounded by the Tibet autonomous region of China in the north and India in the south. It has a total area of 56,139 square miles with a population of 19.7 million people.

Although 85% of Nepal is mountainous, it can be divided into three geographical regions: the towering Himalayan mountain range, the cool terraces and valleys that form the Middle Hills, and the warm, humid lowlands of the *terai* ("teh-RAI").

Opposite: **Nepal is the home of the Himalayas, the tallest and youngest mountain range in the world.**

Below: **The subcontinent of India used to be part of southern Africa, Australia, and Antarctica. The movement of the Earth's crust over millions of years pushed it apart to fuse with the Asian continent.**

THE HIMALAYAS

Along trade routes in the mountains, caravans of horses are used to transport goods from one town to another. The steep and rugged geography of Nepal makes it very difficult and impractical to build roads.

"Himalaya" comes from two words in Sanskrit, one of the oldest languages in the world. *Hima* means "snow" and *alaya* means "abode." This is not surprising as the Himalayan mountains are covered with snow throughout the year. The range stretches across the whole northern part of Nepal.

About 33% of Nepal is at altitudes over 10,000 feet. Almost 10% of Nepal's population lives in this area, subsisting as traders, herders, and farmers. Few crops can grow here: barley, millet, and potatoes are the main ones. These grow up to about 14,000 feet.

The climate is very cold with heavy snowfalls, especially in winter. There is less oxygen in the air, and people arriving from the lowlands will have trouble breathing. Some people develop altitude sickness, which can be fatal unless they go back to a lower altitude.

MOUNT EVEREST

In the entire world there are only 14 mountain peaks over 26,247 feet, and eight of the 10 highest ones are within Nepal, including Mount Everest, the highest mountain in the world at 29,022 feet.

At different times, different mountain peaks were thought to hold the title of highest in the world. Dhaulagiri, Kanchenjunga, and Gauri Shankar (a tall mountain visible from the Kathmandu Valley) were all thought to hold the crown.

Everest was not confirmed as the highest mountain peak in the world until 1863, after a survey done by the Indian Survey Office (at that time, India was ruled by Britain). On the Tibetan side, Everest is called Chomolungma, and on the Nepali side, Sagarmatha. Both names mean "mother of the world." The surveyors, unaware of these names, first called it Peak 15, and then Everest, after a former head of the survey office.

Everest remained unclimbed despite numerous attempts until Sir Edmund Hillary and Tenzing Norgay, a Sherpa guide, finally climbed it in 1953. In 1978, Rheinold Messner and his partner Peter Habler were the first to climb it without using bottled oxygen.

In the mid-'80s, Everest's position as the highest mountain in the world was challenged when a geographer claimed that Mount K2 in Pakistan was higher. Measurements using lasers and satellites confirmed Everest is the highest, and further measurements in 1993 made possible the most accurate measurement ever.

A typical village in the Middle Hills. Terraced fields have been carved out of the hillsides for growing rice, barley, beans, and millet.

THE MIDDLE HILLS

Fifty percent of Nepal is an area called the Mahabharat Range, or the Middle Hills. Calling them hills is a little deceiving, because almost anywhere else in the world they would certainly be called mountains. About half of Nepal's population lives here.

The tops of these hills vary from about 5,000 to 12,000 feet (Mount Whitney, the highest point in the continental United States, is 14,494 feet tall). Seen from the air, the area is a series of endless steep ridges. Over the centuries, steep terraces for growing food have been built wherever possible.

The rugged landscape makes it almost impossible to build roads. Nepalese almost always travel by foot. Distances are not measured by miles, but by the hours or days it takes to walk to a destination. Everything in the meager stores, the few books in school, and the scanty medical supplies, comes in carried on the backs of men, women, and children.

The Middle Hills

The Middle Hills, once crowned with thick, luxuriant forests, are becoming more and more barren. Villagers depend on the forests for fodder, firewood, and building materials. The increasing population has forced them to cut trees faster than they can be replaced. Unfortunately, the loss of foliage causes village water supplies to dry up, and soil erosion eats away at the hillsides.

There are several large valleys scattered among the hills. The largest one is the Pokhara Valley in central Nepal, while the most famous one is the Kathmandu Valley, 124 miles to the east of Pokhara.

Ask people in the Middle Hills traveling to Kathmandu where they are going, and chances are the answer will be, "Nepal." For many, Kathmandu is Nepal.

A picturesque Nepalese village. Life in the village is very difficult. There are no telephones, health clinics, electricity, running water, or other modern facilities.

THE KATHMANDU VALLEY

The Kathmandu Valley has always been the heart of Nepal. It is not very large, about 450 square miles, and now is home to about 1,000,000 people.

The valley lies at almost the exact latitude of Tampa, Florida, but its elevation of 4,383 feet gives it a milder climate. Temperatures rarely go above 86°F in the hot season and even in the coldest months of winter, daytime highs are about 66°F.

The city of Kathmandu, the kingdom's capital, has a population of over 300,000 people and is also home to the king and queen of Nepal. It was founded by King Gunakamadeva in the eighth century. The name Kathmandu was derived from a temple within the city called Kasthamandap, built in the 10th century.

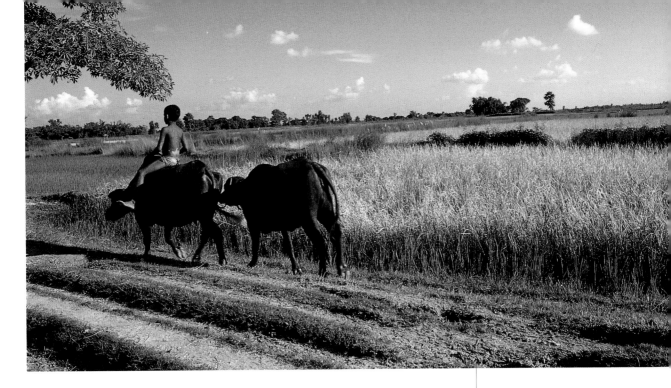

THE TERAI

The only flat part of Nepal is a narrow strip along its southern border with India. It is called the *terai*. Because it forms part of the flood plain of the Ganges River in northern India, the *terai* is very fertile.

However, it used to be covered with thick jungle and was uninhabitable because of malaria, a disease spread by mosquitoes. In the 1950s, the World Health Organization (WHO) sponsored a program to spray large tracts of the *terai* with a pesticide known as DDT. The malaria was brought under control, and settlement of the area by hill people was encouraged.

The *terai* quickly changed into Nepal's bread basket and rice bowl. It is also the center for what little industry Nepal has.

Today, the *terai* is home to over 40% of the population, although it forms only 15% of Nepal's land area. Every year, people from the Middle Hills migrate here at an increasing rate.

The climate in the *terai* is extremely hot, with temperatures in the summer (April to June) reaching 100°F. A deadly wind called the *loo*, with temperatures of over 112°F, sometimes kills people in the fields. The heavy monsoon rains from June to September bring cooler temperatures and rains for the rice fields.

Although much of Nepal's rice is grown in the *terai*, there is little mechanization on farms and animals are often used to plow the land.

The melting ice and snow from the mountains is the source of many of Nepal's rivers and streams.

RIVERS

Nepal has thousands of streams flowing off its mountains and hillsides into hundreds of rivers. They rush down along rocky riverbeds, forming rapids and spectacular washes of whitewater. Yet out of those hundreds of rivers, only three are strong enough to cut through the Middle Hills down to the *terai* and on to the dusty plains of India. These three are the Kosi in the east, the Kali Gandaki in the center, and the Karnali in the west.

During the monsoon, the rains swell the rivers to many times their normal size. There are few bridges in Nepal, and many of them are washed away by the waters. Flooding rivers can wash away houses, and even whole villages.

The rivers are often called Nepal's only natural resource. No one argues that there is tremendous hydroelectric potential, but building and maintaining hydroelectric plants in Nepal's rugged landscape is more difficult and expensive than anyone had imagined. That raises the cost of the electricity produced, making it too expensive for most Nepalese.

FLORA

The extremes of altitudes in Nepal create many different climates and environments, resulting in a fascinating variety of flora.

In the *terai,* for example, sal, a hardwood, is the dominant tree and provides excellent timber for building and furniture.

In the Middle Hills, there are pines, alders, oaks, hemlock, and forests of evergreens, junipers, and birches. There, are also many forests of large rhododendron trees in the east and center of the country.

The bright red blossom of the rhododendron tree is Nepal's national flower. One of the most beautiful sights in Nepal is a forest of rhododendrons in bloom, which turn entire hillsides into a blaze of red in the spring.

Nepal's forests provide over 35% of all the energy used in the country. The trees are also used in all types of construction and the leaves provide fodder for the farmers' livestock.

Nepal's forests are in danger. One report says 3% of the forests are disappearing every year. Each year, as more and more hillsides are stripped bare, the soil on the hills is washed away in the monsoon rains. Without this fertile topsoil, nothing can be grown on the hills.

An effort is being made to save trees and replant those cut down, but it takes a generation to replace what is lost in a day. Deforestation is on the rise, and many consider it the most critical problem facing Nepal.

The rhododendron flower is the national flower of Nepal. The rhododendron tree can be found even at 9,000 feet, although the higher they grow, the later they bloom.

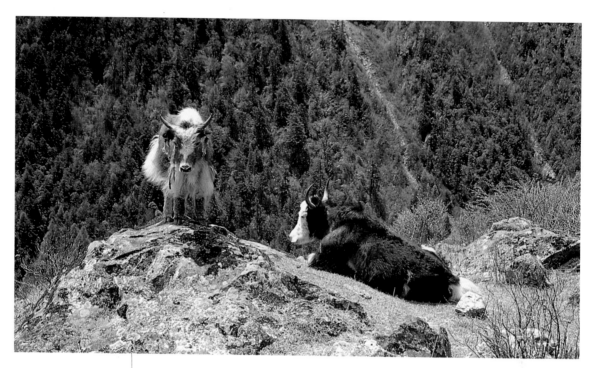

ANIMAL LIFE

In the remaining jungles of the lowlands, especially in the national parks, are Bengal tigers, rhinoceroses, leopards, huge buffaloes, bears, monkeys, and all kinds of smaller mammals. There is also two species of crocodile. Gharials have a needle-nosed snout and will only eat fish. Muggers have big snouts and can be 10 feet long. They will eat anything.

Nepal's most famous and reclusive resident is the rare snow leopard. Little was known about these beautiful silver and black cats until recently. They are solitary and shy and live in the high Himalayan region.

There are ongoing conservation programs to rebuild the populations of tigers, rhinos, and gharials, which are all threatened with extinction.

Not everyone, however, is in favor of the conservation programs. Farmers suffer terrible damage from these animals. Tigers and leopards eat livestock and occasionally a human. Rhinoceroses can ruin a farmer's entire crop in one night. A troop of monkeys will eat through a field in an hour. So it comes as no surprise that most Nepalese feel they are competing with the same animals others are trying to save.

THE YETI

Nepal's most famous resident, the *yeti* (also called the "Abominable Snowman") may not exist at all. The Sherpas, who share its habitat, call it the "yet-tch" and have even distinguished two different types: one that eats cattle and another that eats people.

The *yeti* was dismissed as a legend until a Major Waddell found footprints in the snow in 1899. In 1921, the leader of an Everest expedition reported seeing a dark creature walking in the snow and found some strange footprints.

The *yeti* has managed to elude discovery despite numerous expeditions sent to capture it. The famous mountain climber, Eric Shipton, found a set of footprints in 1951 that prompted several expeditions, including one led by Sir Edmund Hillary, the first conqueror of Everest.

A supposed *yeti* scalp was taken from the Pangboche Monastery for tests and identified as belonging to a mountain goat. Most of the pictures of *yeti* footprints were found to be small bird and rodent tracks that had melted in the sun.

Interest in the *yeti* died down after those disappointments, but when a Sherpa woman was allegedly attacked by one and several of her yaks killed in 1974, interest rose again.

What does a *yeti* look like? Tall, perhaps taller than a person, with orange fur, and a pointed head. Some reports say its feet point backwards. One theory is that it's a giant orangutan species that was thought extinct. Until we actually find one, the *yeti* will remain a mystery, but there is certainly no reason why it couldn't exist.

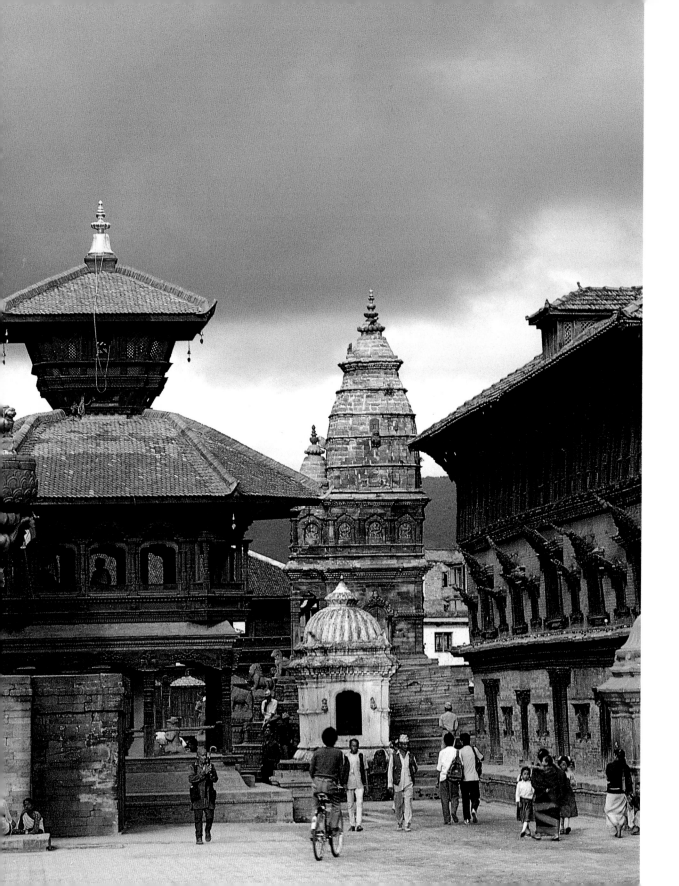

HISTORY

NEPAL'S EARLY HISTORY BEGINS in the Kathmandu Valley. It has become a mixture of fact and legend. The fact is the valley was once a huge lake. Legend has it that the god Manjushri sliced the valley wall at Chohar (where there is a narrow gorge) and drained the water. Geologists tell us the lake drained somehow about 200,000 years ago.

The Hindu god Indra is said to have visited the valley of Kathmandu in the seventh or eighth century B.C. disguised as a human and met with the king. Siddharta Gautama, the founder of Buddhism, was born about 563 B.C. in Lumbini, a town located on the plains of the *terai.* He is also believed to have visited Kathmandu during his wanderings.

Though much of the country's history is shrouded in myth, it is certain that by the time of Nepal's first golden age during the Licchavi Dynasty around A.D. 300, the influence of Hinduism and Buddhism had been firmly entrenched in its society. During those years, visitors from Chinese kingdoms marveled at the architecture and richness of the king's palace and courtyards. When the last Licchavi king died in A.D. 733, Nepal plunged into the dark age of its history.

Opposite: **The splendor of medieval Nepal reflects a history of rich cultural traditions and advanced architectural achievements.**

Above: **A portrait of King Prithvi Narayan Shah. He is known as the "Father of the Nation" because of his military conquests, which united the warring states of Nepal.**

THE GREEN TARA

One of the most significant legacies of Nepal was its introduction of Buddhism to Tibet.

A Nepalese princess, Bhirkhuti, was given in marriage to the powerful Tibetan king, Tsrong Gompo. This man was the strongest, fiercest warrior of his day. He and his army were so feared that even the powerful Chinese sent a princess in marriage as a sign of respect. Bhirkhuti's faith was strong enough to convert the king and Tibet to Buddhism.

Today, Bhirkhuti is still loved in Tibet and worshiped as the Green Tara, symbol of mercy and compassion. She is also worshiped by Buddhists in Nepal.

The pagodas of Patan. In the 16th century, Patan was one of the four rich kingdoms occupying the Kathmandu Valley.

THE MALLAS

In 1200, the Malla Dynasty was established. Although the early Malla kings were strict Hindus, they established a tradition of peaceful co-existence with Buddhists that is still strong today. They were also strong administrators who strengthened and codified the caste system.

For the first three centuries of Malla rule, the valley faced many invasions from western Nepal and the Moslems from northern India. There were as many as 80 small kingdoms in what is now Nepal, all fighting and bickering to increase the size of their tiny kingdoms. Moslems from Bengal did actually overrun the valley in 1364. The Mallas regained control within a week, however, and the short Moslem occupation of the kingdom failed to leave behind any lasting influence.

The Mallas in the Kathmandu Valley prospered, and Nepal's second golden age began in the 15th century. The valley's three main cities, Kathmandu, Bhaktapur, and Patan, grew wealthy on the trade between India and Tibet. Most of the sculptures, woodcarvings, and buildings the valley is famous for today were built during this time.

Yaksha Malla was the greatest of the Malla kings, putting together a kingdom far bigger than the present size of Nepal. His kingdom, however, was divided among his four children. Their quarrels fragmented the small Kathmandu Valley into four kingdoms. Over the next 200 years, each kingdom built fine temples and palaces, but their rulers (all cousins) schemed against one other and eventually caused their own downfall.

Prithvi Narayan Shah's castle in Gorkha. It was from this hilltop fortress that he began the conquest of the Kathmandu Valley.

THE HOUSE OF SHAH

Sixty miles west of Kathmandu, Prithvi Narayan Shah, king of the small Rajput kingdom of Gorkha, watched the bickering of Kathmandu's petty kings and decided to strike. He was brave, a born leader, a good strategist, and a good politician. He was also very persistent; it took him more than 20 years to triumph. Fortunately for him, even after he entered the valley the Malla kings refused to join together. Through battles and political intrigue, Prithvi Narayan Shah conquered the valley's kingdoms one by one. In 1768, he became sole king of the valley.

He and his successors expanded the kingdom until Nepal included Sikkim in the east and touched Kashmir in the west. By the early 1800s, Nepal was one of the greatest powers in South Asia.

21

THE BRITISH

Nepal's expansion brought it into contact with the other expanding power of the time—Britain. In 1814, Nepal and Britain went to war over a territorial dispute. After some initial success on the Nepalese side, the British prevailed. The treaty of 1816 that Nepal was forced to sign reduced the country almost to its present size, and gave Britain the right to keep a representative in Kathmandu.

Forced by the treaty to let the British have a representative in Kathmandu, the Nepalese gave him the worst land in the valley, full of malaria and "evil spirits." They also denied him the right to leave the valley except to go to and from India by a single route.

Nepal was so resentful of foreigners that it closed its borders until 1951.

THE KOT MASSACRE

Nepal's defeat by the British threw the government into turmoil. Members of the aristocracy, all ambitious officers in the army, now had no opportunity to expand Nepal. So they turned against each other and formed factions in a political war for control of Nepal.

In 1846, the queen's lover was murdered during a palace intrigue. The furious queen gathered the various squabbling factions together in her *kot* ("koht," meaning fort), and the accusations and insults flew. Hands reached for swords, and by the next morning several dominant families had been wiped out. Jang Bahadur Rana, one of the faction leaders, survived.

Rana appointed himself prime minister, and he and his family virtually

CHINA

INDIA

ARABIAN SEA

BAY OF BENGAL

NEPAL.

Territory under British Rule in early 19th century.

The British occupation of India in the early part of the 18th century.

Jang Bahadur Rana was the first Nepalese leader to travel to Britain and France in 1850. His family then continued to rule Nepal for the next 100 years.

ruled Nepal for the next 115 years. The king was reduced to a mere puppet on the throne. The Ranas did nothing to improve the country and the lives of the people. When the Ranas were overthrown in 1951, only 5% of the population knew how to read and write.

THE RESTORATION OF MONARCHY

After India's independence in 1947, pressure grew in Nepal for the Ranas to reform the government. There were even protests and strikes at factories in the *terai*. The opposition was led by the able and charismatic B.P. Koirala, who operated from a base in India. But suddenly in 1950, the king decided to seize the initiative. He managed to escape from his bodyguards, sought refuge in the Indian Embassy in Kathmandu, and requested asylum.

King Tribhuvan was flown to India, where he demanded that the Ranas return power to him and the people of Nepal. The Ranas responded by declaring his crown null and void, and appointing Tribhuvan's infant grandson king. All governments refused to recognize the new king and expressed their support for Tribhuvan.

The king and queen toss coins to dancers at a festival. Presently, the monarchy functions only as a figurehead in Nepal.

Tribhuvan declared his support for a democratic government. He became the rallying point for all Nepalese against the Ranas. Popular support for the king soared, and within a year he had taken control of Nepal. King Tribhuvan laid the foundation for parliamentary democracy before his death in 1955. In 1959, a constitution was adopted and all political power was transferred from the king to an elected government.

DEMOCRACY AGAIN

The Nepali Congress Party came into power. But in 1960, after constant friction between the king and cabinet, Tribhuvan's son, King Mahendra, forcibly dissolved Parliament with the help of the armed forces.

Mahendra and his son, Birendra, ruled Nepal with almost absolute power. All political parties were banned. Fundamental rights of free speech and free press were restricted. Local and national legislative bodies functioned as rubber stamps for the king and his representatives.

In the spring of 1979, discontent led to riots in Kathmandu and the *terai*. The king agreed to hold a national referendum on whether to have a

24

multiparty system. The results of the referendum were contested, but the king won by a narrow majority.

Yet, little economic progress was made and many people remained poor and oppressed. Corruption was rampant among public officials.

In 1990, discontent could no longer be contained. After a series of bloody battles between demonstrators and the police in which hundreds of citizens were killed, the king was forced to give up most of his power to a democratically elected, multiparty Parliament.

The Ranas used the wealth of Nepal to benefit themselves by building palaces and living a life of luxury. This Rana palace has since been converted into a college dormitory.

GOVERNMENT

FROM 1959 TO 1960, Nepal enjoyed a brief spell of democracy. However, disputes between the monarchy and cabinet led the king to dissolve Parliament and amend the Constitution to obtain absolute power. In 1990, the monarchy under King Birendra was forced to give up that power and legalize political parties. An interim government ruled until free elections were held on May 12, 1991. The Congress Party won a majority in those elections, and its leader, B.P. Koirala, became prime minister of the Parliament. The main opposition comes from a coalition of Communist parties.

"Nepal is like a yam between two boulders [China and India]."
— Prithvi Narayan Shah

ADMINISTRATIVE ORGANIZATION

Nepal is divided into 14 *anchal* ("AHN-chehl") or zones. In the east and far west, these zones are narrow and run from the southern to the northern border. This means that each zone contains a chunk of the Himalayas, a large slice of the Middle Hills, and a sliver of the *terai*.

Each zone is further divided into a number of *jilla* ("JILL-lah") or districts. There are a total of 75 districts in Nepal. Each district is divided into nine blocks called *ilaka* ("ee-LAH-kah"). The *ilaka* are divided into village committees.

Opposite: **The Nepalese flag is shaped like two pennants, with the sun and moon on the top and the sun alone on the bottom.**

The village committees replace the *panchayat* ("pehn-CHAH-yeht"), the basic unit under the old government. Each village committee elects a chairman, whose duties are similar to those of a town mayor. The citizens also vote for members of the district Assembly and the national Parliament.

Nepal's government had always been highly centralized. Local governments had little authority to pass legislation or control budgets. The new government has pledged to give more power to local authorities under a decentralization program, but in a conservative country like Nepal, change happens very slowly.

Civil servants in Nepal wear the *dara-sarwal* (dah-rah SERH-wahl"), the traditional male suit, beneath a Western-style jacket.

PEOPLE POWER

Except for the brief democratically elected prime ministership of B.P. Koirala in 1959, Nepal has always been governed by a strong figure who came to power either by birthright or force, or both. The king *was* the government. Everyone was ultimately answerable to the king; the king had only himself to answer to.

Pro-multiparty democracy demonstrations began in early 1990, inspired by the revolutions in Eastern Europe. The demonstrations gained momentum quickly in the major urban centers, and at one point government offices were abandoned as civil servants joined the protesters in a march near the palace.

The government tried to put down the opposition, but even though the police fired on demonstrators, the protest marches grew bigger. When dozens of protesters were killed as they approached the palace, the demonstrators threatened to become violent too. The government was almost paralyzed by the time the king went on the radio in late April and agreed to give up power and allow the establishment of a multiparty government.

After tense negotiations during which the he tried to maintain control in the name of national unity, King Birendra finally agreed to the new Constitution, which called for a freely elected Parliament. The prime minister is chosen from the political party in control of the legislature. The two main parties are the Nepali Congress and a coalition of seven Communist parties.

With democracy comes political rallies. Here, members of the Marxist-Leninist party parade the streets.

THE ELECTIONS OF 1991

Four main political parties contested for the 205 seats in the House of Representatives: the moderate Nepali Congress Party, which came into power at the last elections in 1959; the United Marxist-Leninist Party, which represents the Communists; and two monarchist parties, both of which are called the National Democratic Party.

The Nepali Congress Party won a majority of seats. The second-place Communists formed a strong opposition. After decades of hardship, the government is under tremendous pressure to improve the economy and the standard of living. To cut costs, the government has eliminated the jobs of thousands of civil servants. Nepal's people now see that democracy does not mean immediate betterment, and that there is a long, difficult struggle ahead.

ECONOMY

BY ANY MEASURE, Nepal is one of the poorest, most underdeveloped countries in the world. The per capita income is only about $180 a year. This makes Nepal one of the five poorest countries in the world.

Nepal's geography, its lack of almost any natural resources, and its high population growth rate make improving its economic situation very difficult.

There is a huge income distribution gap, too. About 47% of the national income goes to only 10% of the population. The poorest 40% of Nepalese earns only 10% of the national income. Over 90% of Nepal's labor force are subsistence farmers. That means they are only able to grow enough to feed their own family, with nothing left over to sell.

In many areas of the Middle Hills, farmers cannot even do that, and food must be imported from the *terai* or other countries. To make ends meet, men in the Middle Hills are forced to migrate to the *terai* and to India to work as laborers for a few months each year. Earning minimal wages, they make just enough to get by until the next year.

Many young men aspire to be Gurkha soldiers in the armies of India and the United Kingdom. Two vital sources of cash in rural areas are the pensions of retired Gurkhas and the salaries active servicemen send home.

A career as a soldier is highly respected and frequently the only chance to escape a life of poverty. A soldier's salary is often the only source of income the family has. Unfortunately, the United Kingdom is cutting the size of its Gurkha units.

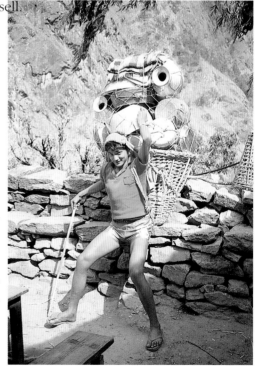

Opposite: **A farmer plows his fields to feed his family, hoping that there may be something extra to sell in the market.**

Below: **All goods are transported through the hills on the rugged backs of porters. Development comes slowly due to the lack of roads, electricity, and other industrial necessities.**

A group of Nepalese women planting rice near the town of Pokhara. Rice is the staple food of the people.

AGRICULTURE

In Nepal, agriculture depends on altitude, because changes in altitude affect the climate. Rice, for example, can only be grown up to about 6,500 feet. Corn, wheat, and millet can be grown higher up, to about 9,000 feet. In the highest altitudes (up to about 14,000 feet), people depend on barley, buckwheat, and potatoes.

Agriculture depends on water, too. Irrigation is usually necessary to grow rice. The higher the altitude, the fewer the sources of water and the harder it is to grow rice. Below 2,100 feet, in the *terai,* it is often possible to grow two crops of rice a year.

Principal crops in Nepal are rice, wheat, corn, millet, buckwheat, barley, potatoes, sugarcane, lentils, and jute. The fertile *terai* produces a sizable surplus, but Nepal still cannot feed itself and must have food aid to feed the people in the Middle Hills.

A Nepalese girl weaving carpets. The Tibetan carpet industry has become an important sector in the export economy of Nepal.

INDUSTRY

Until the mid-1980s, Nepal's leading export was jute, a fiber spun from the jute plant and used mainly for burlap bags. Recently, Tibetan/Nepalese woollen carpets have become Nepal's main export, and the carpet industry continues to grow rapidly. These are mainly exported to western Europe.

Nepal's leading industry, carpets, was begun by Swiss relief workers in the 1960s working with three Tibetan refugees, the only people who really knew the traditional designs and techniques. It was intended to help the thousands of refugees fleeing Communist China's takeover of it.

In the mid-1980s, the carpets became very popular in Europe, particularly Germany, and the industry grew faster than anyone had foreseen. Traditional designs are now being replaced by computer-generated ones, and traditional colors by more popular colors.

Almost no heavy industry exists in Nepal. Jute, sugar, cigarettes, cotton textiles, cement, and leather goods are Nepal's main products. Most industrial development is in the *terai* and the valleys of Pokhara and Kathmandu. They are the only areas with adequate roads and an adequate supply of electricity.

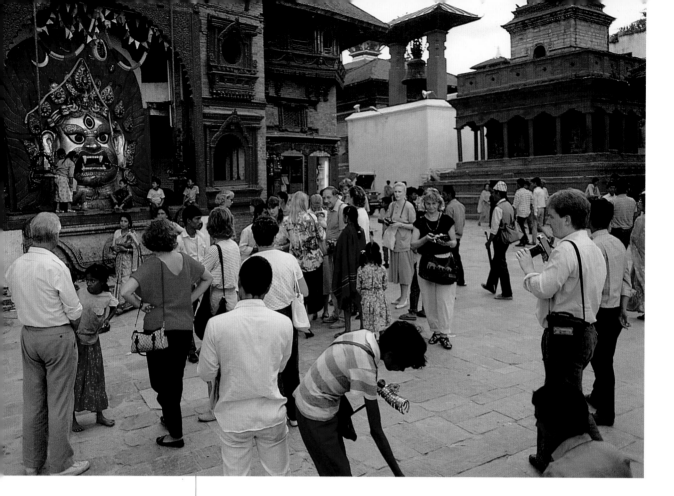

TOURISM

Nepal's biggest industry by far is the service industry that has grown to cater to its tourists. About 200,000 tourists visited Nepal in 1988. After a downturn during the 1990–91 political upheaval, tourism is growing quickly again. Most tourists go trekking in various areas of Nepal each year to enjoy its breathtaking scenery and the ancient culture of its people.

Tourism is often seen as a mixed blessing for Nepal. Studies show that only about 20 cents of every dollar spent by tourists actually goes into Nepal's economy; the rest is used to import basic food and goods.

Since most cooking in Nepal is done on wood fires, thousands of trees are cut each year to cook tourists' food, trees Nepal cannot afford to lose.

Lastly, more and more Nepalese are worried about cultural pollution—young Nepalese abandoning their traditions in pursuit of Western materialism and pop culture.

TRADE

About 50%, of Nepal's trade is with India. The trade balance is skewed heavily in India's favor and shows no signs of improving. The situation is the same overall—Nepal imports about $3 for every dollar it is able to export.

DEVELOPMENT AID

About 40% of Nepal's annual budget comes from foreign sources in the form of grants and low interest loans. Most of this money is designated for development projects; everything from building roads to helping farmers buy fertilizers and vaccinating children. Given Nepal's lack of economic potential, it is likely that aid from foreign governments and institutions will be an important factor for development in the country for many more years.

Many development projects are aimed at improving social conditions. The women here are digging trenches to lay pipes to supply water to their village.

Many governments are giving aid. The largest donor is Japan, and other major donors include India, the United States, Australia, and most of the European countries.

United Nations programs such as the United Nations International Children's Emergency Fund (UNICEF), the Food and Agricultural Organization (FAO), and the WHO are also active. One of Nepal's biggest donors is the World Bank, and there are about 150 non-governmental organizations (NGOs) active in Nepal. NGOs are organizations such as the Red Cross and Save the Children.

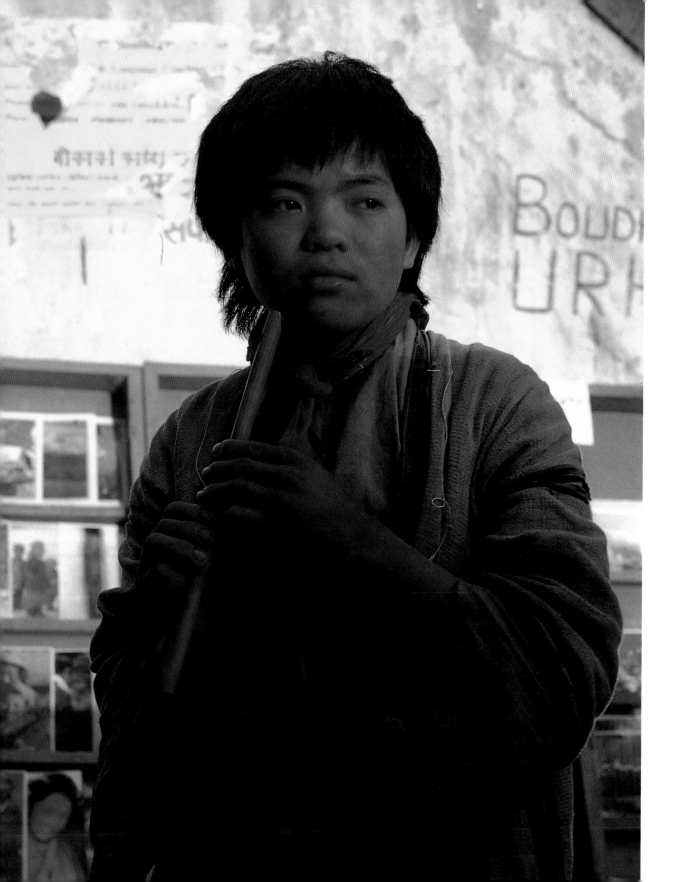

NEPALESE

THERE ARE DOZENS OF DISTINCT GROUPS in Nepal. Even though all these groups have been living together for hundreds of years, there has been little blending or mixing. But there has always been a great deal of tolerance among the different groups.

In Nepal, neighbors may worship different gods and speak different languages, but nobody thinks there is anything strange about that. It is just different. Nepalese like to compare the different ways they live, and the diverse customs of the various ethnic groups are a favorite topic of conversation.

Nepal is a very hierarchical society, influenced by the caste system that originated in the dominant religion, Hinduism, and was codified by the early Malla kings.

The hill tribes are outside the caste system, but have their own class system. Each tribe is divided into a number of clans or family groups and further subdivided.

Nepal's population can be placed into four main divisions: the Hindu caste groups, the hill tribes, the Bhotes, and the Newars.

Opposite: **A beggar boy on the streets of Kathmandu. Poverty has forced many people from the hill tribes of Nepal to seek a living in the cities.**

Below: **The lines on this man's face tell the story of the difficult life in the mountains. Yet the hill tribes remain a very friendly and hospitable people.**

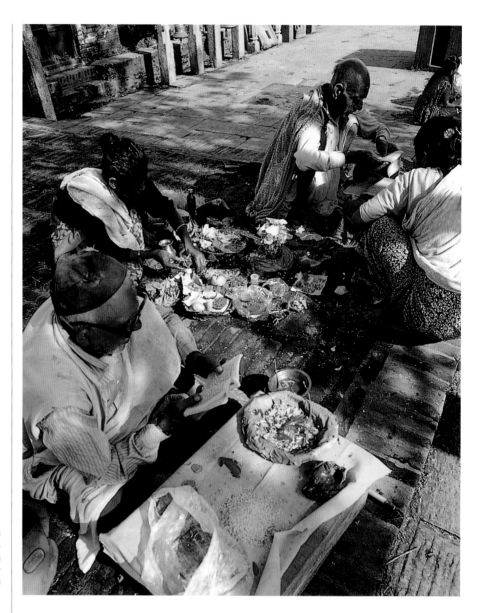

Only people born into the Brahmin caste are allowed to be Hindu priests and carry out the many rites and rituals for the gods.

HINDU CASTE GROUPS

The people of the Hindu caste groups migrated to Nepal between the 12th and 15th centuries when they were pushed from their homes in India by Moslem invasions. They were originally of Aryan stock and have Caucasian features, but with darker complexions. They brought with them their Indo-

Aryan language, which evolved into Nepali, the national language.

The Hindu religion they follow has a strict hierarchy known as the caste system. There are four groups within the caste system: Brahmins ("BRAH-mins"), Chhetris ("Cheh-trees"), Vaisyas ("VIE-siahs"), and Sudras ("SOO-drahs"). Hindus believe humans sprang from the body of Brahma, the god and creator of everything. Brahmins came from Brahma's head and mouth, Chhetris from his arms, Vaisyas from his thighs, and Sudras from his feet.

A group of Chhetri children in western Nepal. These children belong to the warrior caste. Traditionally, they are not allowed to mix with children of lower castes.

At the top are the Brahmins, the priestly caste. They are forbidden by tradition to drink alcohol and eat certain foods like onions, tomatoes, and eggs. A Brahmin must officiate at any religious occasion and are the only group allowed to read the Hindu religious texts.

Below the Brahmins are the Chhetris, the warrior caste. Nepal's king is a Chhetri of the Thakuri sub-caste. Traditionally, many of the Nepal's army officers were Chhetri and even today, many Chhetris join the military.

Only Brahmins and Chhetris have the right to wear the *janai* ("jyah-NAI"), the sacred thread draped across the chest that is the symbol of their high status.

Below the Brahmins and Chhetris are the Vaisyas, the caste of tradesmen and artisans. Below them, at the bottom of the caste system, are the Sudras or occupational caste.

OCCUPATIONAL CASTES

At the lower end of the Hindu hierarchy are the occupational castes. People of these castes take their names from traditional jobs. Some examples are: Kami ("KA-mee"), or blacksmiths, Damai ("dah-MY"), or tailors and musicians, and Sarki ("SERH-ki"), or cobblers.

Today, many have abandoned their traditional occupations and work as porters and day laborers. Ready-made clothes, shoes, and tools make most of their professions no longer necessary.

They are traditionally looked down upon by the rest of Nepalese society and have to endure discrimination all their lives, even from the casteless hill tribes. Most people will not allow people from the occupational castes inside their homes. The occupational castes are at the bottom of the social and economic ladder in Nepal.

A hardworking tailor in a village. Although vital to the community, jobs like these were considered the lowest form of work, and people who did these jobs were looked down upon. These attitudes are slowly changing.

A Magar woman wearing the jewelry common to the hill-tribe women of Nepal. The gold nose pin is called the *phuli* ("FOO-li").

HILL TRIBES

Nepal's many different hill tribes all crossed the high mountain passes to the north or followed the mountain trails from Burma in the east. They all have oriental features and speak their own individual languages.

The hill tribes cluster in villages at higher altitudes of about 6,000 to 9,000 feet. Young men of these tribes predominate in the famous Gurkha soldier units. Although these tribes are casteless, they are subdivided into clans of different status. Gurungs, for example, have four upper clans and 16 lower ones.

Hill tribes practice a religion that is often a combination of Buddhism and Hinduism and sometimes animism. In general, they are less conservative than caste Hindus and more open in their relationships. Teenage boys and girls will openly flirt and court each other, behavior that is almost never seen among their Hindu caste neighbors.

They are generally farmers who also depend on the wool and meat they can sell from the large herds of goats and sheep they keep. For at least part of the year, some members of every family must live a seminomadic life as they take the family's sheep and goats to high pastures at about 12,000 to 14,000 feet during the monsoon.

Young men of the Rai and Limbu tribes of eastern Nepal wear their best for an annual festival. The hat they wear, the *topi* ("TOH-pi"), is the national hat of Nepal.

RAIS AND LIMBUS Also known as Kiratis, these two tribes live all through the eastern hills of Nepal extending across the border into India. The men of these tribes often carry a large *khukuri* ("KU-kree"), the traditional Nepali knife with a curved blade, tucked into a long cloth wrapped around their waist.

The Kiratis are famous for the beautiful stone masonry of their farm terraces. They also build *chautara* ("CHAU-tah-rah"), stone resting platforms topped by large, shady pipal trees, on the trail outside villages as memorials to the dead.

TAMANGS Tamangs are the largest of the tribal groups. They are also the most independent, retaining their own language and Buddhist religion even as other tribes fall under increasing Nepalese and Hindu influence. In Tibetan, *tamang* means horse trader.

Tamangs live in the high hills to the north, east, and west of Kathmandu. They often come to the city to work as porters and day laborers.

The preferred marriage is with one's cross-cousin. For a man, this is his father's sister's daughter or his mother's brother's daughter.

GURUNGS Gurungs live in the hills around Pokhara and east toward Gorkha. They (and the Magar tribe) formed the bulk of Prithvi Narayan Shah's army when he conquered the Kathmandu Valley.

The military is still the main profession of Gurungs. Most families have at least one member serving in India or in the British army in Hong Kong or England.

Those remaining at home turn to farming and goat rearing. From April to September, a member of the family will take the sheep, cows, and water buffaloes to high pastures even above 14,000 feet.

MAGARS Magars live in central and western Nepal, too, but generally farther south and at lower (and warmer) elevations. In the 17th century, they had a very strong kingdom in what is now Palpa, and Prithvi Narayan Shah also depended heavily on them for his troops. Even today, the Magars still send the greatest number of men to the military.

As they are the southernmost of the hill tribes, they have had the longest contact with caste Hindus from India. Consequently, the Magars are the most heavily Hindu-influenced of the hill tribes.

Southern Magars have arranged marriages. The boy's parents send a representative with a bottle of rice beer to the girl's parents. If the beer is accepted, the proposal is approved.

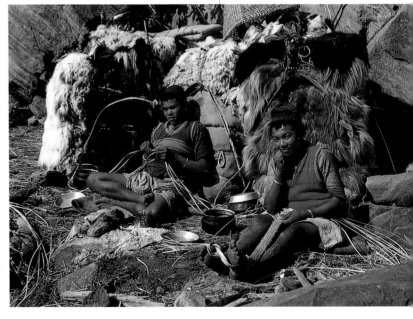

These two Gurung teenagers take a break from carrying their load of goat and sheep skins. They will sell these skins in Kathmandu after a five-day walk from their village.

Above: **Sherpa women are very independent and hold more power than women in Hindu caste homes.**

Opposite: **A Bhote family dressed in all their finery. In the hills where the infant mortality rate is high, families have many children.**

SHERPAS Saying "Sherpa" has become the equivalent of saying "mountain guide" to most tourists, but actually it should only be used for a tribe living mainly in the high valleys of the Everest region in eastern Nepal.

Born at an altitude of more than 12,000 feet at the base of the highest mountains in the world, Sherpas are naturally acclimatized to high-altitude mountain climbing.

Sherpas settled in the Everest area about 300 years ago after crossing from Tibet. They were well-known as traders long before their fame as mountain porters and guides.

BHOTES

All across Nepal's northern border, living in high valleys (with elevations of over 9,000 feet) surrounded by Himalayan mountains are tribes of people called Bhotiya or Bhotes. The Bhote culture is essentially Tibetan *(Bho* is another name for Tibet).

Two of the larger Bhote tribes are the Thakalis and Manangis. These Bhote tribes live in almost total isolation, and each group is usually only as big as small valley where its people live.

All of these tribes are strong Buddhists. They make their living as farmers, sheep- and yak herders, traders, and lately, as hoteliers catering to the incresing tourist trade.

As traders, they travel all over Asia. The Manangis, for example, received special rights for travel and trade from two previous kings of Nepal.

NEWARS

Newars are the native inhabitants of the Kathmandu Valley and have been living there for over 1,500 years. Their language, a mixture of Tibeto-Burmese and Sanskrit origins, is one of the most complex languages in the world.

There are Newar communities in many of Nepal's larger towns. Almost all Newars work as merchants and shopkeepers. It was the Newars who built most of the temples and crafted most of the sculptures Kathmandu is famous for.

Newars have a highly structured caste system dictated over 600 years ago by the Malla kings. As the Kathmandu Valley modernizes, old caste restrictions on occupation are slowly fading. But the social restrictions of the caste system are still largely observed. Newars very rarely marry outside their caste, and those who do risk being cut off by their family and community.

REMOTE TRIBES

There are several ethnic groups that do not fit into any category:

THARUS (see picture) are the indigenous people of the *terai*. Their natural immunity to malaria allowed them to survive in the jungle for centuries before modern insecticides opened the *terai* to other Nepalese.

Living as marginal farmers in settlements scattered throughout the thick jungle, their shyness and lack of experience with money made them an easy mark for ruthless moneylenders, who seized the Tharus' best land when they were unable to repay their debts.

Tharus remain one of the poorest and most exploited groups in Nepal.

CHEPANGS are a tribal group living in the most remote areas of the southern-middle hills of central Nepal. Shy around outsiders, they lived until recently as hunter-gatherers, woodcutters, and sometimes farmers.

They were severely exploited by their better-educated, more aggressive caste Hindu neighbors. The government has started several programs to try to help them.

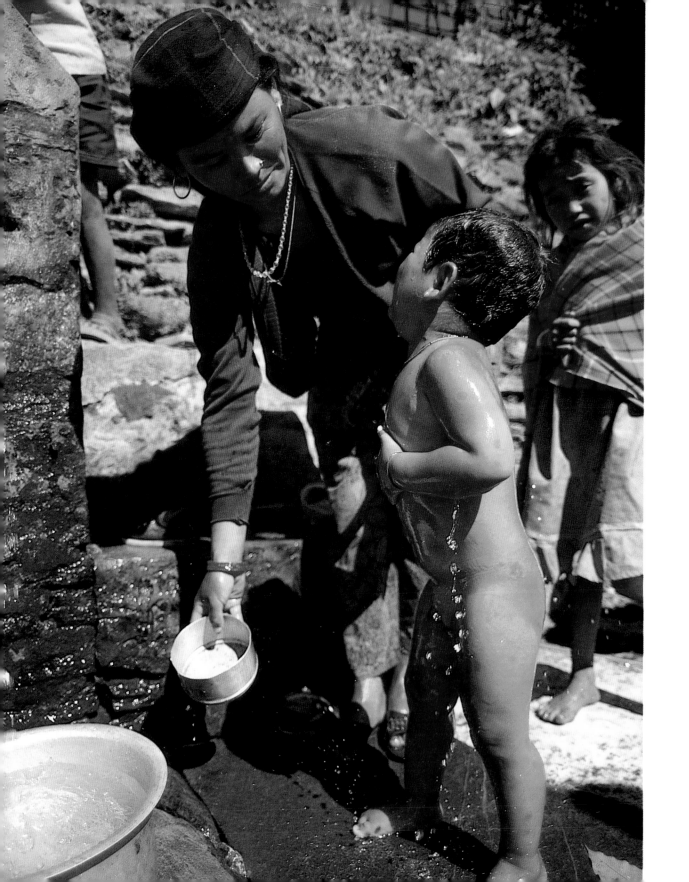

LIFESTYLE

THERE ARE SO MANY DIFFERENT CULTURES in Nepal that the way people think and do things can vary tremendously from one house to the next. Neighbors may speak a different language, worship different gods, even celebrate a different day as New Year's Day. To a Nepalese, this is natural and everyone is extremely tolerant of the different customs practiced around them.

Each cultural group in Nepal has a hierarchical structure. There are divisions and rankings within a family, an extended family, an ethnic group, and society as a whole. This, too, is something Nepalese are comfortable with.

The caste system has been outlawed by the government, but still plays a large role in everyday life. Attitudes are slowly changing, particularly in urban areas, and low-caste people do not carry the stigma they once did. The government is trying to widen opportunities for everyone.

Names in Nepal are traditionally much more than simply names. Names indicate one's caste or group, one's profession, and perhaps, even where one is from.

If one met Mr. Khatiwanda, one would know from his name that he is a Brahmin and probably from western Nepal. Mr. Pokhrel is a Brahmin, too, but from the east. Mr. Sakya is a Newar, and works as a silversmith or goldsmith. As there are many rules regarding interaction between castes, knowing people's name settles the question of whether one can accept the rice they cook or visit their home. But this is no longer as adhered to as it once was.

Opposite: **A child being bathed in cold water. The use of hot water for bathing is almost unknown in the hills where wood for fuel is precious.**

Below: **Leaves and plants are woven tightly together to form a waterproof roof. The leaves also trap the heat to keep the house warm on cold nights.**

FAMILY STRUCTURE

When Nepalese say "my family," they are speaking of a much larger family unit than Americans usually have. Cousins are called brothers and sisters, a mother's oldest sister is called oldest-mother, a father's youngest brother is youngest-father, and so on.

Several generations commonly live in a single household. Sons customarily stay in the home even after marriage, bringing their wife with them.

All the money earned goes into a family treasury that is controlled by the head of the household, usually the oldest male. He has the final say in all important family decisions. This can include which children will study in school, what jobs they can do, and whom they will marry.

Women in Bhote cultures have a stronger position at home and can be very assertive. Their men are away trading most of the time, so the women take over much of the decision-making.

GROWING UP

Name-giving is the first important milestone for the infant in many Hindu homes. Customs vary from group to group, but the name is determined by an astrologer based on the exact time of birth.

Almost all groups have a rice-feeding ceremony called *pausni* ("PAHS-ni") when a baby is about six months old. Many guests are invited for this ceremony and the parents will give a big feast. Guests often give the infant money to wish for its future prosperity.

During a Newar *pausni,* several objects may be placed in front of the baby—dirt, unhusked rice, a brick, toys, a pen, or a hook. The parents and priest predict the child's future talents or occupation based on which object the infant reaches for first.

About the age of five, male Brahmins and Chhetris have their head shaved except for a small tuft of hair toward the back of the head called a *tupi* ("TOO-pi"). The *tupi* indicates that the boy is a Hindu.

Even among the poorest families, children are indulged and spoiled.

PUBERTY

When approaching puberty, male Brahmins and Chhetris receive a *janai,* a sacred thread (actually three loops of cotton twine), worn over the right shoulder and under the left arm. The *janai* is a sign of his high caste and is changed once a year, during the full moon of July or August. After completing this ceremony, he can eat with the men for the first time.

At the age of 12, boys have their heads shaved, are bathed, dressed in saffron robes, given alms bowls, and sent off begging, as the Buddha did thousands of years ago. However, the boys are sent only to their relatives' and neighbors' houses and return home on the same day.

Before they reach puberty, Newar girls go through their first marriage—to a *bel* ("bale"), a wood apple! The *bel* represents the god Subarna Kumar. Since the full marriage rites can only be given once, their subsequent marriage is of secondary importance and they are free to divorce and re-marry.

Newar boys celebrate the onset of puberty with the Bratabhanda ceremony. On this day, the boys will follow in the footsteps of the Buddha and go begging from house to house.

In Hindu and Newar homes, a daughter reaching puberty is no cause for celebration. During her first menstruation, she is locked in a room for 14 days. Considered unclean, she is forbidden to see or be seen by the men of the house or to touch any food but her own. Sometimes even the women of her own house avoid her touch.

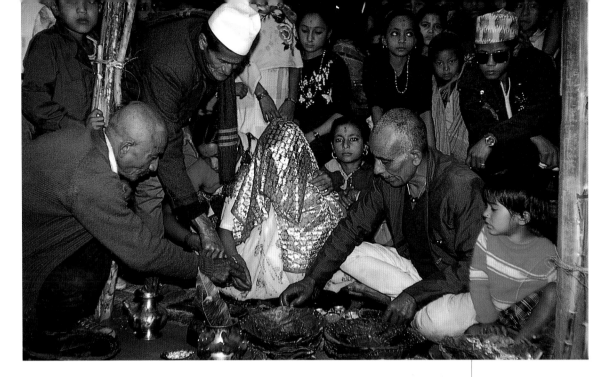

MARRIAGE

Almost all marriages are between members of the same caste or ethnic group. Inter-caste marriages are extremely rare, as both husband and wife will be cut off from their respective families.

The marriages of caste Hindus and the Newars are usually arranged by the parents. A relative of one side acts as a go-between, relaying photos of the boy and girl and conducting the necessary convincing and negotiations. Sometimes the couple is allowed to meet, but only if accompanied by plenty of chaperones.

The hill tribes have three types of marriages. There are arranged marriages, or the boy and girl may court and choose each other, or the boy may capture/kidnap the girl. He then has three days to convince her and after that must release her if she still refuses. Actual wedding customs, though, vary widely from group to group.

Although it is illegal, polygamy still occurs in Nepal. The most common reason for marrying another woman is because the wife is unable to hear a son. All the wives may live in the same household or separately.

Bhotes, because their men are gone for long periods on trading trips, practice polyandry. A woman may marry several brothers at the same time. All children are considered the oldest brother's.

DOMESTIC ARCHITECTURE

Houses in Nepal vary according to the people who live in them and the climates wher they are built. Many people in the *terai* build their homes on stilts and keep their animals below. Living higher is some protection from snakes, animals, and mosquitoes. It is also much cooler and breezier off the ground. Each house stands in its own compound.

Higher up in the hills, where there are fewer snakes and winters are colder, the houses are more solid, with thick stone walls and thatched or slate-tile roofs. Windows are small, without glass panes. There is no chimney for the fire, either. The creosote from the fire coats the wood above and protects it from bugs. Houses are closer together and two or three homes may share a compound.

In the high Himalayan region, people live on the second floor like in the *terai,* but here it is to get away from the cold. That is also the reason why homes share a common wall with their neighbor; there is less chance for the cold to get in. Animals live beneath the house and their body heat helps to warm the rooms above. The houses are constructed of stone and wood, with wooden shingles weighed down by heavy stones.

THE HEARTH

Each ethnic group places special importance on the hearth and cooking area. A non-Brahmin should never enter the cooking area in a Brahmin house. To do so would pollute the area, and a religious "cleansing" ceremony would have to be performed.

A Brahmin male takes off his clothes and wraps a length of white cloth called a *dhoti* ("DHOH-ti") around himself before he steps into the hearth area to eat.

In the Middle Hills and Himalayas, though, a guest will immediately be given the best seat by the hearth—on the right side, near the back wall of the hearth.

Most social activity takes place around the fire, which is in an open pit with an iron tripod where pots are placed. People here, too, respect the hearth and they are careful not to throw anything that could be considered "dirty" into it.

In the northern hills, the hearth is the center of the house. Guests are asked to sit by the fire as soon as they come in.

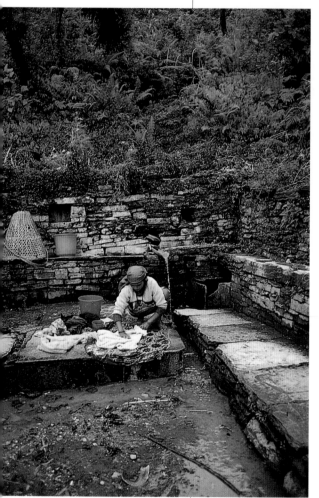

In the villages, many household chores take place outside the house. It is common to do the washing at the nearest spring or river.

A TYPICAL DAY IN THE VILLAGE

Work in the village begins before the roosters crow. There is wood to be gathered, fodder to be cut, and water to be fetched. Water may come from a nearby well or from a stream or tap over an hour's walk away. As the forests disappear, water is disappearing too, and people have to walk farther and farther for both fuel and water.

The fire is lit and cooking starts as soon as the household stirs. There may be tea with sugar, but probably not every morning. Most people eat *derdho* ("DAIR-dhoh")—a mixture of millet, corn, and wheat flour boiled into a thick paste. To go with this, there may be lentil soup and some vegetable curry (potato is most common) or just vegetables with broth. If the family cow or water buffalo has a calf, there may be milk or yogurt.

After eating, some children go off to school, while others help out in the fields or at home. School starts at 10 a.m.

Whether it is farm work, grazing cattle, or getting wood or water, everything is done by hand and carried backs. After school, children may play or join their parents at work.

People use the sun, not watches or clocks, to tell time. As the sun begins to set, everyone gathers around the fire. Light may come from a tiny kerosene lamp or just from the fire. After eating dinner (probably *derdho* again), the family gathers to talk until everyone goes to sleep.

A TYPLCAL DAY IN TOWN

People rise early in town, too. Nothing tastes better than a steaming glass of Nepalese milk tea on a cold morning. Water may be in the house or have to be fetched from a nearby tap. Mother starts work right way because it takes about two hours to cook on her single kerosene stove. She prepares a meal of rice, lentil soup, vegetable curry, and maybe milk, yogurt, or meat. Children get ready for school or play.

Father then goes to his shop or office, and mother begins her housework If parents can afford it, they send their children to private English schools. School buses may be anything from a rickshaw to a rickety old van packed with classmates.

Mother washes the dishes and clothes at the nearest communal tap and then goes to market to buy the day's vegetables and food. There is no refrigerator to store a week's groceries. After school, children play, study, or maybe go see the new Indian movie in town—the cheap seats are only about five cents.

Father finishes his work at 5 p.m. and makes his way home slowly. He talks to friends, maybe over a cup of tea or local liquor, and stops at the newsstand to browse through the latest books and magazines. When he comes home, he checks his children's studies. In each room candles are always handy, in case there is another blackout.

The evening meal is late, 8 p.m. or after, and everyone goes to bed soon afterward.

These schoolchildren happily look forward to playing with their friends after the ride home in a bicycle rickshaw.

57

WOMEN IN NEPAL

Surveys show that women in the village do over 70% of the work. This includes fetching water, fodder, and firewood, hoeing, weeding, harvesting—every kind of work. There are only the most basic tools. Everything is done by hand and everything is carried on someone's back.

A new bride usually lives with her husband's family and must earn the respect of her in-laws through hard work. Though life is not always rosy, divorce is very rare.

Women have almost no decision-making power. Women in caste Hindu homes, in particular, are powerless. Women in Bhote families may be very powerful because the men are away on trading trips so much of the time. Women in the hill tribes are somewhere in-between.

Sons are hoped for; daughters are needed to work in the fields. Because the family must bear large expenses (maybe even a large dowry) when a daughter marries, girls are considered a burden as well as a source of labor.

The Nepalese government is trying to improve the condition of women, but women are still underrepresented and discriminated against in many areas of Nepalese life.

HEALTH CARE

One out of 10 children in Nepal dies before the age of one. Three out of 20 do not survive beyond the age of five. One reason families want many children is because they believe some will inevitably die.

Many of the health problems come from poor hygiene and sanitation. Few houses have toilets. People use the nearby fields or streams and then clean themselves with water using the left hand. Worms and diarrheal diseases are easily spread in this way. Thirty-three percent of child deaths are caused by diarrhea.

The government is trying to provide a hospital in every district and a healthpost in every village committee. Still, it takes hours for people to travel to the healthpost and days to reach the hospital. And once they arrive there, the doctor or medicine may not be available due to transportation and communication problems

Many people still go to a traditional faith healer, called a *jankri* ("JAHN-kree"), if they are sick. The *jankri* supposedly removes the cause of the illness, often by going into a trance while beating on a drum. Some *jankri* do have a great deal of real knowledge about medicinal plants and mix herbal medicines to treat illnesses.

EDUCATION

Going to school in rural Nepal is totally different from going to school in the United States. Students walk to school, and this may take up to two hours. Lessons are conducted outdoors. Classrooms are used only when necessary as they are dark and cold due to the lack of electricity. Few textbooks are available, so students are taught to memorize their lessons.

Nepal's literacy rate today is 37.7%. Considering that in the 1950s the literacy rate was only 5%, Nepal has come a long way despite the difficulties of providing enough teachers and textbooks. Only 23% of the women can read and write.

A typical mud-brick schoolhouse. Before lessons, the students and teachers gather to sing the national anthem and do some calisthenics.

DEATH

Death is treated in different ways in different cultures. Hindus cremate the body by the banks of the nearest river. They pick out a small piece of bone and throw the ashes in the river. They believe that the ashes will eventually reach the sacred waters of the Ganges River in India.

The hill tribes of Magars and Tamangs also cremate their dead, but on top of a hill, not by a river. Gurungs either cremate or bury their dead. A priest decides which, based on the position of the stars at the time of the person's death.

Almost every group in Nepal has elaborate ceremonies to mark the first anniversary of the death. During this ceremony, the family of the dead person gives a large feast for the entire village.

Wood is scarce in the Himalayan region, and so cremation is difficult. Often the land is also too rocky for digging graves. The Bhotes, who live in this area, take the body to a high place, chop it into little pieces, and leave it for the birds to eat.

COMMON COURTESIES AND ETIQUETTE

When Nepalese meet each other or leave each other, they join their hands in front of them in a prayer-like gesture and say *namaste* ("neh-MEHS-tay") or sometimes *namaskar* ("neh-MEHS-kahr"). These are from Sanskrit words, which mean "I bow to the god in you."

Himalayan people drape a thin white scarf called a *khata* ("KAH-tah") around the neck of someone they want to show respect to or of someone leaving on a trip.

Nepalese seldom say *dhanyabad* ("DHAHN-yah-bahd"), meaning "thank you." Nor do people open a present when it is given. To avoid any chance of embarrassing anyone, they open it in private.

The feet are the dirtiest part of the body, the head the most sacred. A Nepalese will never step over a person. If a Nepalese touches you with his feet by accident, he will immediately reach down, touch your feet and then touch his own head as if to say, "I am sorry. Your feet are higher than my head."

Objects should be given and taken with the right hand. Since the left hand is used to clean oneself after using the toilet, it is considered very dirty.

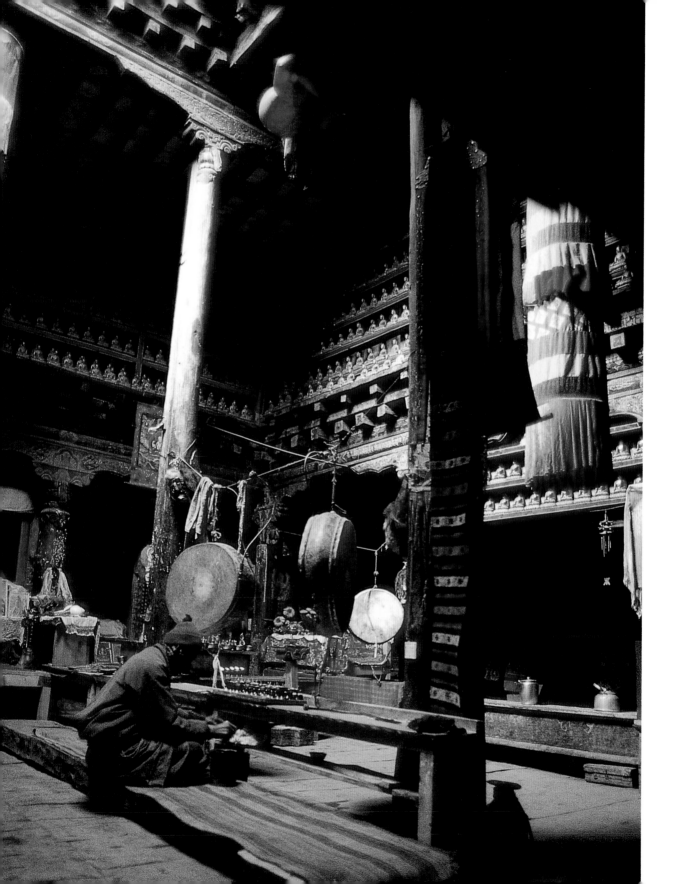

RELIGION

NEPAL'S POPULATION is about 90% Hindu, 8% Buddhist, and 2% Moslem according to the last census. In everyday life, though, the line between Hindu and Buddhist is far from clear. Many people follow both religions. Hinduism, in particular, is a part of everyday life, as it is integrated into daily routines such as shopping or going to work.

Because the Buddha is considered a form of the Hindu god, Vishnu, Buddha's teachings are well-known and have great influence even among Nepalese Hindus.

Opposite: **This Buddhist** *gomba*, **or monastery, was built 500 years ago.**

Below: **A Brahmin priest gives a** *tika* **("TI-kah") to a young girl. The** *tika* **is a sign of blessing and a symbol of knowledge.**

HINDUISM

Hinduism, the oldest living faith in the world, has no person who can be identified as its founder. There is no governing or regulating body, and there is no specific dogma that can be pointed at to say, "this is what a Hindu believes."

The vast body of philosophy from which Hindus define their beliefs is called the *Vedas,* which consists of 1,008 hymns and revelations of saints and seers that was first recorded well over 1,000 years ago.

Hinduism encompasses many beliefs, so many that some directly contradict others. According to Hindu philosophy, there is more than one righteous path to understanding the mysteries of life. It is up to individuals' own capacities, attitudes, and requirements to build their own system of beliefs. To Hindus, all religions lead to the same end. Hindus may even embrace other religions without ceasing to be Hindus.

Hindus believe in reincarnation, that they are reborn after death, moving up or down a universal ladder. Their actions in this life determine their next life. If they are bad, they may be reborn into a lower caste, as animals, or even as insects.

If they do great good in this life, earning much *dharma* ("DHARH-mah") or merit, then their next life will be enriched. After living thousands of lives, they may be able to climb into heaven, released from the cycle of life and death at last.

Their condition in this world and the random things that happen in their lives, are part of their *karma* ("KAHR-mah") or destiny. It does no good to feel anger and rebel against *karma. Karma is* accepted and borne. This attitude of tolerance helps the Nepalese bear their poverty, but it may make motivation for change difficult.

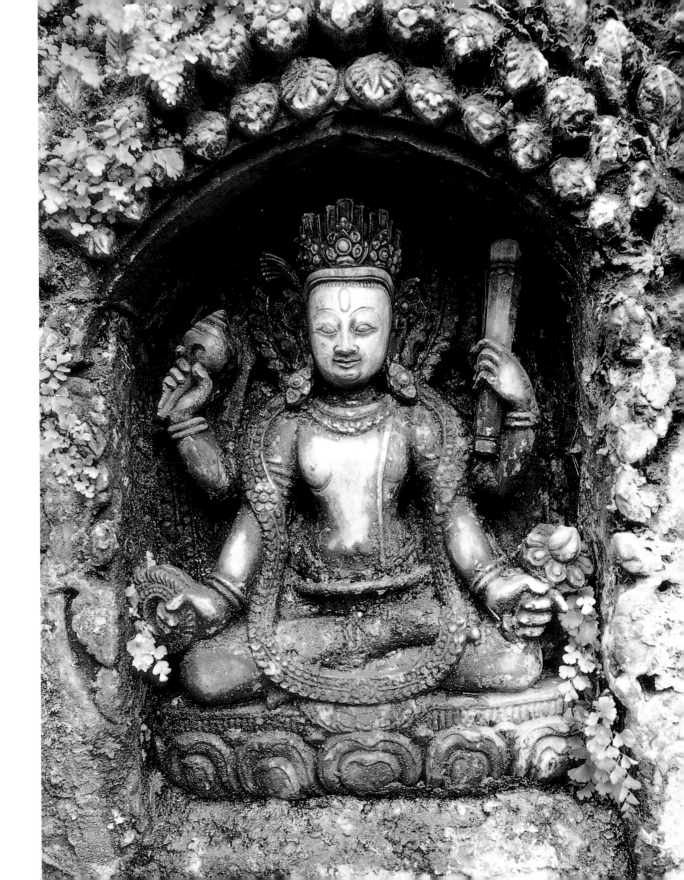

HINDU GODS

One Hindu text states that there are 300 million gods, and Hindus themselves actively worship hundreds. But only three stand out: Brahma the Creator, Vishnu the Preserver, and Shiva the Destroyer. These three gods combine to become Brahman, the ultimate divinity found in everything.

The same god may be called a dozen different names and may be manifest in several different forms. Vishnu, for example, has 10 different forms, including a lion, a dwarf, the Hindu hero Krishna, and even the Buddha. The Nepalese consider the king himself to be a manifestation of Vishnu.

Shiva, with over 108 different names, is the god most worshiped in Nepal. Known as the Destroyer, he is also called the "bright or happy one," and is honored as Lord of the Dance. He is often pictured as an ascetic, his body smeared with ashes and wrapped in leopard skin, wandering far and wide or meditating at his home on Mount Kailash in Tibet. It is believed that the waters of the Ganges River springs from the mat of hair piled high on his head.

Ganesh, Shiva's son, is one of everybody's favorite gods. His father cut off his head by mistake, and to appease his wife, swore to replace it with the first living thing he found—which turned out to be an elephant. With his elephant head and roly-poly body, Ganesh does not look like a typical immortal. Still, he is the god most people would first turn to for their requests.

Durga is one of the forms of Shiva's wife, Parbati. Durga is the goddess worshiped during the festival of Dasain ("dah-SIGH") for her victory over an evil demon.

Laxmi, the goddess of wealth, is appealed to during the festival of Tihar ("TI-hahr").

Saraswati, the goddess of wisdom, is usually portrayed riding a swan and playing a sitar.

Indra, the god of rain, is prayed to during the monsoons.

BUDDHISM

The Buddha's real name is Siddhartha Gautama. Buddha (an honorary title meaning "enlightened one") was born around 623 B.C. in Lumbini, which is now part of Nepal's *terai*. Born into a rich and perhaps noble family, he lived a life of luxury and ease in several palaces.

Being curious about life outside, he made several secret trips outside the palace. Shocked by the pain, death, and suffering of the people, he decided to renounce everything, even his wife and son, to try to understand what he had seen.

For the next six years, he went through every form of deprivation as he meditated and searched for the answers to life. Finally realizing them, he became the Buddha. For the rest of his life he walked with a group of disciples, talking with anyone who listened or asked and spreading his message. He died at Bodh Ghaya in India.

White prayer flags are hung outside temples and monasteries as the people believe the winds will carry their prayers to heaven.

All Buddhists believe that life is a cycle of birth, death, and rebirth in a wheel of life. One's rebirth is based on one's *karma,* which is the sum result of one's actions, words, and thoughts in life. A Buddhist's goal is to break the cycle of rebirth by living a life of self-detachment and deprivation. If a Buddhist does this, he or she attains *nirvana* (release from life). Several Buddhist schools have evolved since the Buddha's life thousands of years ago. The Theravada school is followed in Sri Lanka and Southeast Asia. The Mahayana school has influenced Tibet, Nepal, and north Asia.

THE TEACHINGS OF BUDDHA

Today, in Lumbini, there is a small temple on the spot where Buddha was supposedly born, but little else to commemorate him. Brick ruins of monasteries that were built 1,000 years ago stand in the tall grass and there is a mound and pillar built in 250 B.C. by Ashok, the great Indian emperor. The Buddha's teachings, though, spread throughout Asia to Japan, Indochina, and even the ancient kingdoms of Indonesia.

THE FOUR NOBLE TRUTHS

1. In all our lives there is pain from disease, suffering, birth, and death.
2. The basic cause of these lies in our desires for material things, for pleasures, and for people.
3 Detachment from these desires ends pain and provides an escape from the cycle of rebirth.
4. The eightfold path is the way to attain this detachment.

THE EIGHTFOLD PATH

Right understanding, right thought, right speech, right action, right livelihood, right effort, right mindedness, and right concentration.

One important difference between the two schools is that in Theravada philosophy believers are only concerned with their own release from the cycle. The Mahayana says that those who find the way must "go back" and help others do the same.

A woman spins a prayer wheel. These objects help those who are unable to read or recite the Pali scriptures of Buddhism.

IN DAILY LIFE

Each morning in Nepal the streets are full of people going to the neighborhood shrine for *puja* ("POO-jah"), meaning "worship. Each carries a tray with colored powder, flower petals, some grains of rice, a few small sweets, and a small bell. All this will be used in worship at the temple.

Many people encountered in the morning will have flower petals in their hair. This is part of *prasad* ("prah-SAHD"), the blessing received from the gods in return for worshiping them. The mark many people wear on their forehead, the *tika* ("TI-kah"), is another sign of blessing, symbolizing the third eye of inner wisdom and vision.

They believe divinity is in everything; in themselves, in the plants and animals and even in the rocks. Roads are built around large rocks and trees rather than removing them and risk disturbing their divinity. Thus it is impossible for the Nepalese to separate their daily lives from religion as what they do and say affects them in this life and the next.

Hindus worship the cow as their Divine Mother and also as a symbol

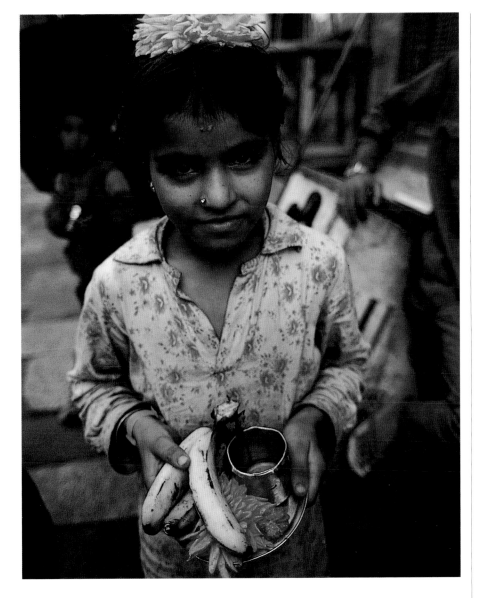

A young girl on her way to the temple. The food is donated to the gods as an offering or *puja*.

of fertility. The cow's products and byproducts, milk and yogurt, even dung and urine, have special religious significance. A Hindu would never think of killing a cow or eating beef. Cows wander loose everywhere. They have good reason to feel secure: the penalty for killing a cow, even by accident, can be up to 20 years in jail!

Both father and son are Moslems. They can be recognized by the skullcaps on their heads, which are of Middle Eastern origin.

OTHER RELIGIONS

About 2% of Nepal's population is Moslem. Almost all Moslems live in the *terai*. In some places they are in the majority. There is a very small Christian population. In certain remote corners of the Himalayan area, Bon, the Tibetan religion before Buddhism, is still followed.

In the face of cultural and religious diversity, the Nepalese exercise great tolerance and mutual respect for the beliefs of others. They are proud of the fact that there has never been any religious conflict in Nepal.

FOLK BELIEFS

There are customs, superstitions, and rituals, both large and small, to cover almost all aspects of everyday life. Because of Nepal's cultural diversity, customs which are important or offensive to one culture may be nothing to another. Here are some customs and beliefs:

Never blow out a light with your breath; wave something, even just your hand, to fan out the flame.
After lighting a lamp or just switching on an electric light for the first time that day, a Nepalese will make a *namaste* gesture toward the light.
Fresh water should be fetched every morning; water that stands overnight is considered no longer clean.
Before serving food, a little rice will be placed in the fire as an offering to the gods.
When you see a baby for the first time, give some money (a rupee or a few coins) to guarantee its future prosperity.
If a bee hovers near you, good fortune is coming, too.

The Nepalese travel often, and there are a whole set of beliefs about travel:

If your feet itch, you will be traveling soon.
Some people take a betel nut, a coin, and some rice wrapped in a cloth to ensure a safe trip.
It is unlucky to start a trip on a Tuesday.
It is unlucky to leave under a new moon.
A large jug full of water on each side of the doorway ensures a safe trip.
Try not to come back on Saturday.

Mothers threaten their naughty children with, "the foreigner will come and eat you!" but the Nepalese had enough strange creatures and spirits even before foreigners started arriving:

A *jhumi* ("JHYOO-mi") will grab you and lead you away from your house without your knowledge if you leave early in the morning without telling anyone.
If you meet a beautiful young woman late at night, look at her feet. If they're pointed backwards, run! She's a *kichikinni* ("ki-chee-KIN-nee"), the spirit of a dead woman.
A *mulkatta* ("mool-KAHT-tah"), a dead man's spirit, wanders around headless.
If you wake up, but don't feel you can get up, it's a *khya* ("Khi-yah") holding you down. If a *khya* gets upset, it tickles you to death.
Pret ("preht") and *pisach* ("pi-SAHCH"), unhappy spirits, wait at crossroads and cremation sites to chase people and make them sick.

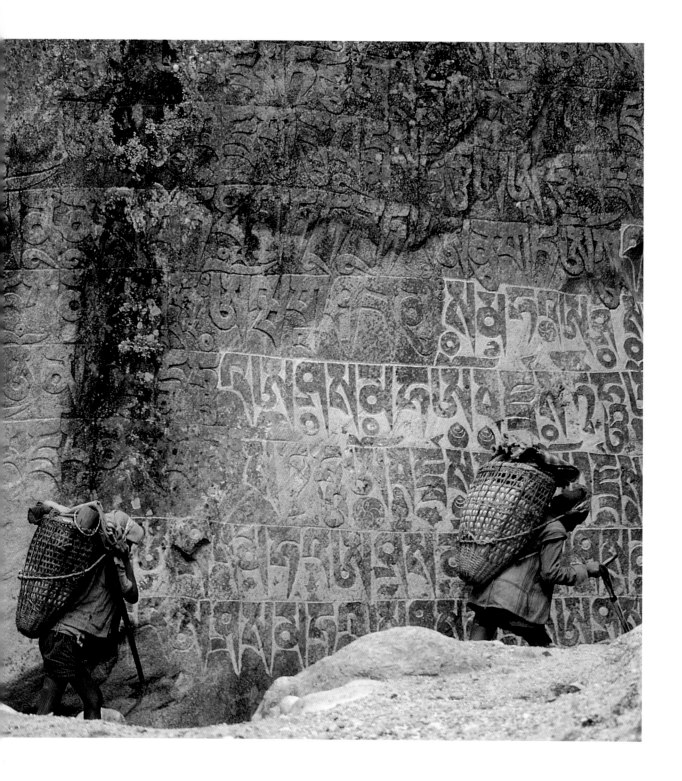

LANGUAGE

THERE ARE OVER A DOZEN LANGUAGES spoken in Nepal and each language has many different dialects. In fact, dialects change with almost every ridge you cross. For example, a Tamang from Dhading in central Nepal will have a hard time understanding a Tamang from Taplejung in the east. This is Nepal's geography at work again.

Nepali is the national language and the one people from different groups use with each other. Nepali is an Indo-European language and has many similarities to the Hindi language of northern India. Nepali and Hindi share the same script and have many similarities in grammar and vocabulary.

THE NEPALI LANGUAGE

Nepali sentence structure is very different from English. The usual order is subject-object-verb. There are "markers" to identify the words which are the subject, object, or indirect object. The marker for the subject is *le,* for indirect object the marker is *laai.* For example:

> Ramle Sitalaai paani diyo.
> Ram to Sita water gave.
> (Ram gave water to Sita.)

There are two different verbs that share the function of the English verb "to be." One form is used when describing something that is so at that moment, while the other is used for permanent state of beings.

Nepali also has some sounds that English does not have. For example, there are two "d" sounds, while English has only one. Nepali also has several aspirated sounds—like an extra "h" to a sound. This is very difficult to hear and pick up. For example, "ka" and "kha."

LANGUAGE AS ETIQUETTE

The Nepali language can be very formal and polite. The words one uses will change according to whether one are talking to a friend, a shopkeeper, one's parents, or a high official. There is even a separate vocabulary used only when speaking to the royal family.

The words used when talking to people depends on their status relative to the speaker. Higher words are used for people one should show respect to and lower words for people who should show respect to the speaker. That means children talking to their parents will use one vocabulary to ask them a question, but the parents will use another form to answer the children.

It is the same at work. Bosses will use words and forms that definitely let subordinates know who's the boss. But with their own superiors, bosses will use words that show respect.

WRITING

The Devanagari script is very old. It is the same script used to write Hindi. Each character represents a sound, not a letter. Words are formed by joining the characters with a line across the top. The Nepalese write below the line on lined paper.

Nepal is a nation of linguists. It is common for even young children to speak at least two or three different languages. Most children start out speaking their own group's language at home, then learn Nepali in school. They usually pick up Hindi as they grow up. In school, they also study English.

THE DIFFERENT PERSONS IN YOU

There are many different ways to say "you," depending on the respect you should give, or want to give, the person you are talking to:

yaahaa —("yah-HAH") Very polite.

hajur —("hah-JOOR") Polite, often used by women when talking to their husband.

tapaai —("tah-PIE") The most common form used in everyday conversation with casual friends or shopkeepers.

timi —("TI-mi") Used with good friends, children, or lower caste people, sometimes used by a husband with his wife. It can imply affection, or a sense of superiority, or both.

ta —("tah") Used with animals, young children, people of very low status, or someone you want to fight with. It can imply great affection, or a total lack of respect.

OTHER LANGUAGES

The languages of the hill tribes and Bhotes are called Tibeto-Burmese languages. They are a little like Chinese and are monosyllabic and tonal. To speak correctly, the right stress and tone must be used, either rising or falling. The same syllable may have several meanings based on the different stress used in saying it.

The Bhote languages in particular are very close to Tibetan and use the Tibetan script.

Newari, the language of the Newars, is an Indo-European language that has absorbed a great deal of influence from Tibeto-Burmese. It is one of the most difficult languages in the world to learn.

In the *terai,* there are a great number of Indo-European languages spoken. The two most widely spoken languages after Nepali are Bhojpuri and Maithili. These are very different from Nepali. Although the languages have common roots, a Nepali speaker and a Maithili speaker will have a very difficult time understanding each other.

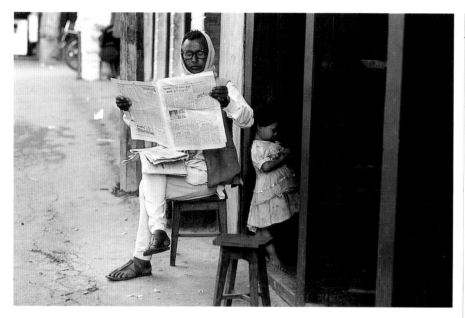

NEPALESE PROVERBS

What's something totally insignificant? It is "a cumin seed on an elephant's trunk." The Nepalese have all kinds of proverbs and sayings, which reflect the world they live in. Some of them are easy for us to understand, others require a little reflection:

> He can't face a live tiger, but he'll pull the whiskers off a dead one.
> He couldn't see a buffalo on himself, but he'll find a louse on someone else.
> Too many cats kill no mice.
> If you need a drink, you have to find a spring.
> Give someone a drink, but don't show them the spring.
> No one sits by a burnt-out fire.
> A knot tied with a laugh is untied with tears.
> Dress according to the land you are in.
> It takes a hundred more lies to hide the first.
> The sun can't be covered by your hand.
> The carpenter's staircase is broken.
> The elephant went through, but its tail was caught.

ARTS

IN KATHMANDU IT IS EASY TO WALK PAST a 1,000-year-old statue without even knowing it. As daily life swirls around, masterpieces in wood, stone, metal, and brick are treated with the casualness of an old friend. Sometimes it is hard for us, used to hushed, pristine museums, to understand. Great works of art are as much a part of daily life and routine as the morning cup of tea. To Nepalese, their art is not to be locked away and viewed from a distance on special occasions; it is an ingredient in their daily environment, to be touched, sat on, worshiped, or even used to entertain little children.

Nepal's greatest fine arts are in the forms of sculpture and architecture. There is almost no secular art. Almost all Nepalese art is generated for worshiping the two great religious traditions that shape so much of life in the country, Hinduism and Buddhism.

And Nepalese art is mostly anonymous. We know the names of the patrons, but not the names of the artists and craftsmen who executed their commissions.

Not so with music. By far the favorite subject is romance, and songwriters are household names. Children are brought up to sing and dance without embarrassment, and when they get older their ability to sing with wit and dance with grace might help them attract and win the heart of that special someone.

In a country largely free of television and radio, Nepalese still rely on each other for entertainment.

Opposite: **A dancer and his mask. The arts in Nepal were performed for the pleasure of the gods. The lure of money from tourism has led to mass production of Nepalese art.**

Below: **The *garuda* ("gah-ROO-dah") is a mythical bird from the religious drama, the *Ramayana* (rah-mah-YAH-nah"; see Page 86). *Garuda* can be found in other Asian countries of Hindu influence, but no single sculpture really looks like another.**

A group of Newar musicians move in procession as they play during a religious festival.

MUSIC

The Nepalese love music. Walk through any village and you are bound to hear someone singing, the lilting sound of a flute, or the catchy rhythm of a drum. Radios are becoming more common, but still, in most places in Nepal, if you want to hear music, you make it yourself.

A wedding would not be possible in Nepal without a band announcing the approach of a wedding party. In the far west, the band is mostly drums. In the Middle Hills, people blow the *shanai* ("shah-NYE"), an oboe-like instrument, and big horns that curve back and over. In the cities, bands with Western instruments blast out Western and Hindi pop songs in a style that is half-polka, half-Dixieland, and all fun.

The hymns and religious songs sung at temples are accompanied by drums, large cymbals and tiny finger ones, flutes, and harmoniums. In Buddhist monasteries high in the Himalayas, lamas on rooftops play huge horns that are 10 to 15 feet long. Their low bass rumble echoes through the high mountain valleys and can be heard for miles.

SONG

Singing is almost a national sport in Nepal. At many festivals in the Middle Hills, a singing competition is always one of the main attractions.

There are two teams, boys and girls. One side sings a short verse, asking rhetorical questions, criticizing the other side's song or dress, or telling a story. As the one side sings, the other must think up a wittier and more poetic reply. Onlookers offer judgments. Highest marks go for the wit of the verses. The sides may go back and forth all night, ending with an agreement to meet at the same place, same time next year.

On of the great traditions of Nepalese music, and one that is fast disappearing, is *gaini* ("GUY-ni"). *Gaini* are wandering minstrels who travel from town to town and literally sing for their supper. They sing of famous old stories as well as the latest rumors and gossip. They live on the donations from the crowd of villagers who gather to listen. Long ago, a whole family used to travel together, the son learning the songs at his father's knee. These days, *gaini* are slowly fading away in the age of radios and Walkmans.

There are nationwide competitions every year for folk songs. The wit and poetry of the verses are at least as important as the melody and singer's voice.

This is a religious dance performed only once every 12 years. The masks represent the many different gods and goddesses.

DRAMA

Traditional dramas retell the great adventures of the *Ramayana* and *Mahabharata* (mah-hah-bhah-REH-tah"). These dramas are performed during religious festivals and sponsored by neighborhood religious organizations.

There is also a burgeoning modern drama movement. These are mainly social dramas about the new problems confronting Nepal's increasingly urban, Western-influenced population: youthful alienation, evil schemers, drugs, and even topics such as the position of women in society and corruption.

Comedy has a long tradition in Nepal, and no drama would be complete without a comic interlude or two, sometimes even three. In recent years, comic reviews have toured the larger towns and been a big success.

The biggest comic event of the year occurs during the Gai Jatra festival. Held at the Royal Academy in Kathmandu, it is the one day of the year when you can poke fun at anything or anybody, no matter how big or powerful they are. There are no rules; anything can be said and no one can take offense. The results are uproarious, and cassette recordings of the evening are always bestsellers.

DANCE

Religious dances are very common in Nepal. The dancers wear elaborate costumes and huge masks and headdresses. Their dances depict the struggles and triumphs of the gods over demons. An example are the dancers of the Indra Jatra festival, who walk through the streets and dance at the temples and the old palace.

Buddhists have a strong tradition of religious dance, too. Twice a year, in the Mount Everest area, the Sherpas hold a three-day epic dance re-enacting the triumph of Buddhism over the old Bon religion. People from all over the world come to see the elaborate costumes and masks, and the controlled energy of the dancers.

Almost every ethnic group has its own folk dance style. Himalayan people put their arms around each other's shoulders and form a sort of chorus line. Rai and Limbus hold hands (both men and women) and dance slowly in a circle.

In caste Hindu culture, men and women rarely dance together. Women rarely dance at all. Traditionally, one or two men will dance surrounded by a close circle of people singing, clapping, and urging on the swirling dancers.

In this Gurung village, two young girls dance the story of a long deceased king and queen. Sadly, with the influence of pop culture, many young people are turning away from local traditions.

These Brahmin priests are singing and reciting verses from a religious song they have published. They will try to sell these to the crowds who have gathered to hear them.

LITERATURE

Nepal is also a nation of poets. There are a number of poetry competitions throughout the year. These are often broadcast over the radio, and with the start of television to some areas in the late 1980s, the finals are shown on the screen as well.

The birthdays of the most famous poets are celebrated with parades and recitations of their poems. Prasad Devkota, who lived from 1909 to 1959, is considered one of Nepal's greatest poets. The royal family also writes poetry. Several of the queen's poems have become popular songs.

Brahmins, members of the religious caste, sometimes privately publish a booklet of long poems they have written. They recite the poem in public, singing it to a simple melody and sell the booklets to the audience gathered to hear them. These poems are usually religious homilies, using a story to make a point from Hindu scriptures.

THE *MAHABHARATA* AND THE *RAMAYANA*

The Hindu epics combine the teachings of the *Vedas* with great stories and legends. They have been entertaining and teaching children and adults alike for thousands of years. Children can still recount the adventures of their favorite heroes.

Like the Greek *Iliad,* the stories have a basis in history, with the gods and goddesses playing an active role in the affairs of man. The *Mahabharata* recounts the heroic struggle of five brothers, the Pandava, against their five evil cousins. Within the *Mahabharata,* the *Bhagavad Gita* (Song of God), presents the essence of Hinduism.

The *Ramayana* centers on the adventures of the great hero Ram, his wife Sita, and his brother Laxman. Sita is kidnapped by the terrible demon Ravenna. After much searching, Ram's friend, the monkey king Hanuman, finds her on the island of Sri Lanka. Following a terrific battle, Ram finally kills the demon and rescues Sita with Hanuman's help.

Nepal figures in both epics. The great Nepalese king, Yalambar, is killed in the *Mahabharata*'s climactic battle. In the *Ramayana,* Ram wins the Sita's hand in marriage in a competition in Sita's home, Janakpur, in Nepal's *terai.*

PAINTING

The Buddhist "wheel of life" is painted in the Tibetan style and is called a *thangka*.

There are two main painting traditions in Nepal, one with its roots in the south, the other in the north. Paintings, too, are mainly devoted to religious themes.

Showing southern influences are Newari paintings from as far back as the 11th century. These are miniatures to illustrate manuscripts, and the style is derived from Indian work. By the 15th century, Brahminical manuscripts were being beautifully decorated by miniatures similar to an Indian style called *pahari* (pah-HAH-ri"). These painters were all Chitrakars ("CHI-trah-kerhs"), the painters' caste in the rigid caste system used by the Malla kings.

From the 14th century, Nepalese painters started to work on scrolls inspired by Tibetan scroll paintings called *thangka* ("TAHNG-kah"). *Thangka* are religious paintings of Buddha and other Buddhists themes such as "the wheel of life." Nepalese artists traveled to Tibet and across Central Asia and brought this new art form back to Nepal.

Today, Tibetan *thangka*-style paintings are becoming well-known and popular in the West. Rich in color, elaborate in design, and extremely detailed, their appeal is easy to see. Newari paintings, called *paubha* ("POW-bah") or *pati* (PAH-ti"), document all aspects of religious life, but for the most part have not caught on in the profitable tourist market.

SCULPTURE

The greatest period of sculpture came under the Malla kings from the 15th to 17th centuries. Most sculpture was made to decorate the palaces and temples and was shaped by Newar craftsmanship. Being a sculptor was not considered a respectable profession. The people who did these beautiful statues were not considered worthy of noting, and so the names of any of these master artists are not known.

Sculptors worked with wood, stone, and metal (usually brass). There are stone sculptures from as long ago as the sixth century, and the wooden sculptures on some of the temples are more than 900 years old.

Nepalese sculptors liked to work with metal best of all. They used the lost wax method: making a wax model to make a clay mold, both of which are destroyed when the statue is actually made. Another popular technique was *repousse*. This means using a hammer and chisel to tap and pound a design into a sheet of metal, usually copper.

Both of these methods are still in use today. Visitors walking down the streets of Patan will hear the clinking sound of hammers tapping on metal.

Craftsmen still work in the traditional manner. A large share of the work is aimed at the tourist market.

ORIGINS OF THE PAGODA

At the end of the 13th century, a master Nepalese architect, known today as Arniko, traveled north at the invitation of the Tibetans. As he and his team of 24 assistants completed several projects, Arniko's reputation spread and came to the attention of the Ming emperor of China. Arniko joined the court of the emperor and today, one of his buildings stands in Beijing. The style of pagodas seen today all through East Asia owes its origins to this remarkable and little-known man.

ARCHITECTURE

Religious architecture is Nepal's main contribution to world art. Seven places in Kathmandu Valley have been designated world heritage landmarks by UNESCO. No other place in the world has so many important landmarks in such a small area.

Much of Nepal's architecture is the world of Newar craftsmen working through the 17th century. Builders and craftsmen were paid from the state treasuries, and no expense was spared. They built with brick, wood, and stone. Today, the palace squares remain much as they were centuries ago. Most of these architectural treasures can still be marveled at in the Durbar squares of Bhaktapur, Kathmandu, and Patan. These squares contain the royal palaces of the old kingdoms.

The same cannot be said for the old neighborhoods of the valley. The old brick and tile buildings are rapidly being replaced by concrete and corrugated tin.

In the 19th and 20th centuries, the Rana prime ministers filled Kathmandu with huge European-style palaces. Today, the largest of their palaces are government offices and hotels.

All over Buddhist areas of Nepal you will find structures that are half-sculpture, half-architecture, called *stupas* ("STOO-pahs"). *Stupas* are Buddhist shrines. Two of the largest and most beautiful are at Bodhanath and Swayambhu in the Kathmandu Valley.

Stupas are Buddhist representations of the universe. The mound represents earth, water, air, and fire.

The eyes are those of the Buddha, the third eye is the eye of true knowledge, the nose is the number one and represents unity.

The 13 rings of the spire are the 13 degrees of knowledge, and the ladder to *nirvana* ("nir-VAH-nah") is represented by an umbrella-like structure at the top.

LEISURE

LIFE IN NEPAL moves at a slower pace than it does in the United States. There are no shopping malls, and most stores are only a single small room, often no bigger than a closet. There are none of the luxury goods, so taken for granted in the United States, to put in the stores anyway.

Television affects only a small portion of the population in Kathmandu and the *terai* and only broadcasts for a few hours a day. There is only one radio station, and it broadcasts for only part of the day. There are parks and sports fields only in a few cities. Tennis courts, for example, are found in only three places within the country. Reading material is scarce.

What do people do when they are not working? Mostly people just relax and hang out, talking to friends, listening to other people talking to their friends, sipping a cup of milk tea in the village tea shop, and watching people walk by.

Some lie down in a cool, shady spot and take a nap or just sit under a tree doing nothing, waiting for a friend to come by in order to discuss the latest village gossip.

Above: **Bhaagh-chaal** ("bahg-chahl") is a form of Nepalese chess with pieces in the form of tigers and goats. Usually, though, stones are used as a substitute as people cannot afford to buy a set.

Opposite: At Namche Bazaar, the sale of clothes and food attract crowds of Sherpas to this once-a-week market.

Left: Soccer is regularly played in the more urban areas of Nepal but is not popular in the hills because of the lack of flat land.

95

MOVIES

People in Nepal love to go to the movies. Every large town with electricity will have a theater of some kind. Movies are a great bargain: even the best seats are only about 30 cents. Most of the movies are from India and are in the Hindi language. Many Nepalese speak Hindi, which is very similar to Nepali.

Even the smallest understanding of Hindi is enough in order to enjoy the movies. The plots are simple and direct—the bad guys are really bad, the heroines arebeautiful, and the heroes are all almost supermen.

Movies last about three hours and have a little bit of everything—tragedy, comedy, rock'em-sock'em fights, and spectacular musical numbers—and often switch from one to the other in the space of a few seconds. The seats may be backless benches, the theater may be as hot as an oven, and the projector bulb may blow every 10 minutes, but movies are still great entertainment.

Video is bringing movies to even the most remote villages. Porters will carry a TV, a VCR, and a small generator for days through the hills, turning the school hall of each village they come to into a temporary theater. The entire village will turn out to watch. For many, it is the first movie they have ever seen. At first they cannot even understand the images on the screen, but like anywhere else, they quickly become critics.

MODERN SPORTS

Volleyball is the most popular sport in the hills because it does not require a large playing field. In the *terai* and larger valleys, soccer is also popular. There are several national club tournaments, and teams from all over Asia are invited to take part. Cricket is played in some large towns.

In the 1988 Seoul Olympics, a Nepalese boxer won Nepal's first and only Olympic medal ever, a bronze. The martial arts, particularly tae-kwon-do, are becoming very popular, and Nepalese players are now strong contestants in all-Asian competitions.

TRADITIONAL PASTIMES AND SPORTS

With no money to spend on elaborate equipment, most Nepalese games only need what can be picked up from the ground to play.

One of the most popular children's game is *dhandi-biu* ("DHAHN-di byoo"). A bat-like stick is used to flick the end of a small seed lying on the ground, flipping it into the air. The player tries to tap the seed twice while it is still in the air, and then hit it as far as possible. The farthest hit wins.

Kite flying is also popular. Nepalese kites have no tails and control is difficult. Once up in the air kites fight each other. The goal is to use the kite's string to snap the string of your opponent.

Nepal's most famous game is called *baagh-chaal* (tiger and goats, played on what looks like a Chinese checkers hoard). The object of the game is for the tigers to eat up all the goats by jumping over them onto an open space, or for the goats to trap all the tigers by preventing the tigers from moving.

The traditional national sport is *kabaddi* ("KAH-bahd-di"), which originated in India. Two teams of boys face each other across a line on the ground. A player from A team rushes across the line and attempts to tag one of the players on B team, all the time saying "kabaddi." The players on B team try to avoid the tag, but if one of them is tagged, they rush to stop their opponent from recrossing the line. If they can hold him till he runs out of breath and stops yelling "kabaddi," they win. He wins if he recrosses the line. There is a similar game for all-girl teams. National tournaments for both sexes are held every year.

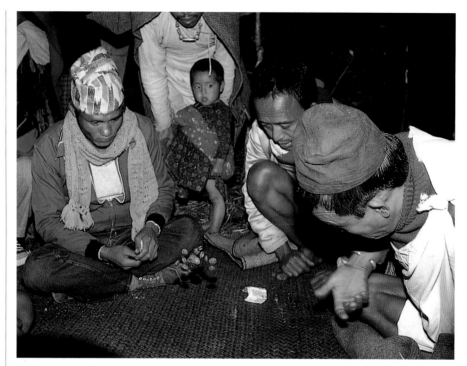

Opposite: **The biggest one-day *mela* is held at Tribeni on the banks of the Narayani River. Over 100,000 people gather to bathe during the full moon in February.**

Right: **Gambling is a regular feature at the *mela*. Here, the men bet on which way the walnut shells will land when thrown.**

THE MELA

Strictly local festivals called *mela* ("MAY-lah") are a main source of local entertainment and leisure. *Mela* are religious celebrations held annually. The date of the *mela* is based on the phase of the moon, usually at full moon or new moon, or halfway between. Nothing much happens at the *mela* except that people have a good time.

Often, people will walk for days to go to a good *mela*. At the *mela*, people get a chance to see friends from other villages whom they have not seen for a long time, to eat foods they cannot always find, and to buy some clothes or jewelry. Men gamble, women gossip and shop. Young people sing, dance, and court, and small children do not worry about bedtimes. These days, no one is surprised if a porter carries in a VCR and generator. A two or three movies will be shown repeatedly for as long as fuel for the generator lasts.

Mela can last between a day to several days. Each community in an area will have its own *mela*, providing entertainment at intervals throughout the year. Usually *mela* are held beside or near rivers or streams.

FESTIVALS

Nepal has dozens of festivals. If you include local festivals, it is safe to say that there is a festival every day somewhere in Nepal. Although there are some secular holidays, all the major holidays and festivals are based on some religious celebration.

Many are dedicated to the worship of a specific god or goddess. Shiva Raatri ("SHEE-vah RAH-tree"), for example, is dedicated to the Hindu god Shiva. Some have a more human emphasis. Bhai Tika ("bhye TI-kah") is a festival between members of a family, and Tij ("teej") is for women only.

Because of the differences between Hindus and Buddhists, what is a festival for one group may mean nothing to another. Dasain ("dah-SIGH"), the biggest Hindu holiday, is nothing to Buddhists. Losar ("LOH-sahr"), New Year's Day and the year's biggest holiday for the Himalayan people, is not celebrated by the rest of the population. Indra Jatra ("IN-drah JAH-trah") is only observed in the Kathmandu Valley.

Usually, each area will have its own festival once a year. These festivals are a combination of a religious celebration and a county fair. Overnight, small stalls selling food and trinkets will spring up in an open field. People will walk all day, celebrate, eat, sing, dance, and gamble all night, then walk back home. The date for such *mela* depends on a particular phase of the moon in the same month each year. The largest is the Tribeni Mela held under the full moon each February. Over 100,000 people gather for this one-day fair.

Opposite: At the Raato Machhendranath festival, this woman seer waits for a customer. She is consulted for advice on suitable marriage dates and partners.

Below: A joker in the Gai Jatra Festival. During this event, people are given the opportunity to poke fun at just about anything.

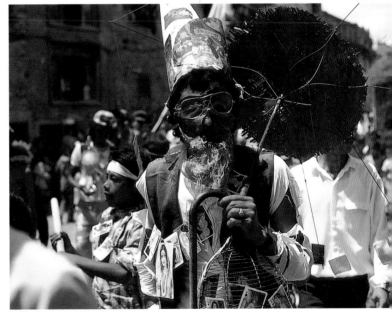

A FESTIVAL CALENDAR

The dates for festivals are determined using Nepal's lunar calendar and the dates change annually on the Gregorian Calendar.

December-January	Seto Machhendranath The Holy Month of Magh
February-March	Shiva Raatri—Lord Shiva's Night Tribhuvan Jayanti
March-May	Baleju Jatra Ghora Jatra Biskhet Jatra Mother's Day Raato Machhendranath Buddha Jayanti—Buddha's Birthday
May-August	Mam Rimdu Naga Panchami—Day of the Snakes Janai Pumima—the sacred thread
August-September	Gai Jatra Krishna Jayanti—Krishna's Birthday Father's Day Tij—Women's Festival
September-October	Indra Jatra Dasain Tihar
November-December	Sita Bibha Panchami Bala Chaturdasi

TIHAR—THE FESTIVAL OF LIGHTS

Tihar feels very much like Christmas. There are gifts, decorated houses lit at night, special foods, and even a special nocturnal visitor: Laxmi, goddess of wealth and good fortune.

Five animals are worshiped during Tihar. On the first day, housewives leave food out for crows. On the second day, dogs are given flower necklaces and *tika* and fed at a banquet. Cows, symbols of Laxmi, are bathed and garlanded on the third day, bullocks on the fourth, and people worship each other and themselves on the last.

During the festival of Tihar, the cities and towns are ablaze with lights to guide the goddess of wealth to people's homes.

At midnight of the third day, Laxmi visits deserving houses. Homes are cleaned, and tinsel and lights or oil lamps are placed everywhere. A path is painted and adorned with oil lamps from outside the door to where the home's valuables wait for the goddess' blessing. Beside them are a burning lamp, some flowers, and food for Laxmi. Excited children set off fireworks.

Women of the neighborhood go singing from house to house and are rewarded with presents. On the following night, it is the men's turn.

On the fourth day, homes are lit again and Newars celebrate their New Year's Day. The fifth day is most important. All over Nepal, brothers travel to visit their sisters to receive Bhai Tika ("Bhye TI-kah"), meaning "brother's blessing." This blessing is so important that if a boy does not have a sister, a relative will act as a sister. In return for the blessing, the sister receives gifts of cloth and money.

During the festival of Tij, women dress in bright red *sari* after having their ritual bath in the river.

TIJ—FESTIVAL FOR WOMEN

Even though it means fasting for at least a day, women in Nepal look forward to the three days of Tij, the only festival they can call their own. It is their only break from household duties. On the first day, women of the house eat a fine feast, sparing no expense as they must fast on the second day.

The fast replicates one done by Parbati as she prayed that Shiva would marry her. Shiva did marry her, and in return, Parbati promised that any women who fasted would have a good marriage and many children. All day, groups of women gather by rivers and streams.

After bathing, they dress in their best clothes, usually a bright red *sari* ("SAH-ree"), and worship Shiva. Then they gather with friends and neighbors to sing and dance into the night.

On the morning of the third day, each woman makes an offering of food to her husband and breaks her fast. A ritual bath ends the festival.

SHIVA RAATRI—SHIVA'S NIGHT

Each February, tens of thousands come to bathe in the Bagmati River at the point where it flows by Pashupati Temple in Kathmandu Valley. Devotees come from all over India and Nepal on the 14th day of the waning moon, the anniversary of a night long ago that Shiva spent here in meditation.

Shiva is said to love the spot so much that he returns on the same night each year to meditate. By spending the night in meditation and bathing at dawn, you gain great favor with the powerful Lord Shiva.

In February, the temperature may be 32°F and the water is freezing cold. Bathing is no easy thing to do. The woods near the temple becomes a huge campground, lit with the fires of thousands of pilgrims chanting and trying to keep warm through the long night.

At the first light of dawn, people start bathing in the icy river. They stand in line for hours to pour a little of the river water over a stone *lingam* ("LING-gum"), a fertility symbol representing Shiva.

People throng to bathe along the river of Pashupati Temple to celebrate Shiva Raatri.

105

THE KUMARI

The Kumari is believed to be the goddess Kanya Kumari in human form. The Kumari is chosen at the age of about four from the Sakya clan of gold- and silversmiths.

Her body must have 32 special signs and cannot have any flaws or scars. She must identify items known only to the Kumari. Lastly, she must walk fearlessly through a dark room filled with men in demon masks and bloody buffalo heads. If she passes all that, she is the Kumari, the Living Goddess.

She moves into a palace, and while she lives there like a queen, she is forbidden to leave except for a few special occasions. Even then, she is carried because her feet must never touch the ground.

She remains the Kumari until she loses blood, either from a cut or upon reaching puberty. Then she returns to her own family, an ordinary person again. Many ex-Kumaris find this transition from divinity back to being a mortal very difficult to make. For some, being the Kumari becomes a stigma, not a blessing.

INDRA JATRA

The eight-day Indra Jatra is the main festival of the Kathmandu Valley. Long ago, Indra, the god of rain, came to the valley to steal some beautiful flowers he saw from high above. He was caught by the people and tied in heavy ropes like a common man. It was not until Indra's mother came to seek him and convinced the people of Indra's true identity that they released him. In return, she gave the people two gifts. She would take to heaven all who died that year and she gave the valley the wet, foggy winter mornings that help moisten the crops even now.

Indra Jatra is also used to worship the terrible god, Bhairav ("BHYE-rahv"), the destroyer. Every neighborhood puts a mask of this terrifying deity on display and worships him. The climax of this celebration begins at night when, from a large mask of Bhairav, rice beer flows out and crowds of young men wrestle for a drink.

During the festival, beautifully costumed and masked dancers wander through Kathmandu, re-enacting the search for Indra.

For three nights, the Kumari ("koo-MAH-ree"), the Living Goddess, is drawn through the streets in her chariot. On the second night, as thousands wait, the Kumari gives a *tika* to the king. This rite symbolizes the goddesses' blessing on the king, and continues prosperity for the kingdom.

From the huge mouth of a Bhairav mask, rice beer is released. Somewhere in the flow is a small fish. To drink it is to have guaranteed prosperity for the next year.

DASAIN

Dasain is as important to Nepalese Hindus as Christmas is to Christians. All offices and stores are closed for most of this 11-day celebration. Nepalese will do anything they can to be home for it. All workers receive a bonus. Special foods are made and everyone gets a new set of clothes.

Dasain celebrates the victory of good over evil, represented by the victory of the goddess Durga ("DUR-gah") over the demon Mahisasura ("mah-hee-sah-SOO-rah"), who terrorized the earth in the form of a huge water buffalo. Durga, the wife of Shiva, is pictured riding a tiger or a lion, her arms filled with the weapons she used to defeat Mahisasura, who lies prostrate at her feet.

On the first day, each household plants barley seeds. On the ninth, each household sacrifices an animal, (fowl, goats, or even a water-buffalo) by slitting the throat or beheading it with a large *khukuri*. The blood from the animals is dripped over all vehicles, from bicycles to jet planes, to ensure Durga's protection for the coming year. The sacrifices are followed by a big feast.

The actual victory of Durga over the demon is celebrated on the 10th day. Everyone puts on the new clothes bought for Dasain and visits relatives and friends to exchange greetings and *tika* on this day of joy. On the 11th day, the barley, which has grown into bright green sprouts, is distributed by the head of the household and worn on the head as a sign of blessing.

The Goddess Durga rides her tiger as she triumphs over evil. Nepalese celebrate her victory during Dasain, the biggest festival in Nepal.

Once a year, the Raato Machhendra is pulled through the city and believers rush forward to touch it and pray for good fortune.

RAATO MACHHENDRANATH

("RAH-toe mah-CHEHN-dreh-naht") Each year, the great god Raato (red) Machhendra is taken from his temple placed in a wagon topped by a 40-foot spire of pine-covered bamboo, and pulled through the narrow streets of Patan. The wagon stops in each and every neighborhood to give everyone a chance to worship. The Nepalese believe that the Raato Machhendra controls the monsoon rains, so it is vital to keep him happy.

It can take a month or more to travel through the city. Very often, the wagon collides with houses, the spire threatens to fall over, and the wheels get stuck in gutters, among other things. Each neighborhood and village takes a turn in supplying the hundred or so men necessary to pull the wagon.

The climax comes in an open field where the king comes to display a sacred vest given ages ago by the Serpent King to the Raato Machhendra for safekeeping. It is believed that the continued presence of the vest guarantees plenty of rain for the coming rice-planting season. Tens of thousands cheer as the king holds the vest high for all to see.

BUDDHIST HOLIDAYS

LOSAR The most important festival in the Himalayan areas is Losar, or New Year's Day. It is a time for dressing up in new clothes, visiting family and friends, and lots of eating and drinking.

At Bodhanath near Kathmandu, big crowds string prayer flags from the *stupa*. A photo of the Dalai Lama, the spiritual leader of Tibetan Buddhists (and exiled secular leader of Tibet) is carried through the crowd.

At the climax, an exact moment determined by astrologers, everyone hurls handfuls of *tsampa* ("SAHM-pah") flour (flour made from roasted barley) into the air, then at each other. Groups of people form long lines, with arms over each other's shoulders, and dance in a slow shuffle.

BUDDHA JAYANTI ("Buddha JYAIN-tee") On the full moon of April or early May, the birth of the Buddha is celebrated throughout Nepal's Buddhist community. People make trips to a monastery, where lamas hold special services, and there are feasts and visiting of friends and relatives. In Kathmandu, Swayambhu Temple is the center of the celebrations, with thousands climbing the 300 steep stairs to the top to worship at the many shrines around the *stupa*.

These color badges are for the festival of Raksha Bandhan. The sister ties the badge around her brother's wrist as a sign of affection.

FESTIVALS OF THE FAMILY AND HOME

DASAIN and **BHAI TIKA** are festivals that combine the worship of a god and goddess with a celebration that strengthens family ties. There are several other festivals too which are mainly to strengthen the ties between family and home and primarily celebrated within the family.

MOTHER'S DAY, known as "Aamaa-ko mukh herne din," literally meaning "see mother's face day." All children, even those that have married and moved away (usually daughters), return home. They present sweets, fruits and other gifts to their mother and bend down to touch their forehead to her feet as a sign of respect. Mother places her hand on their forehead as a sign of blessing.

FATHER'S DAY, "Buaa-ko mukh herne din," is celebrated in much the same way as Mother's Day.

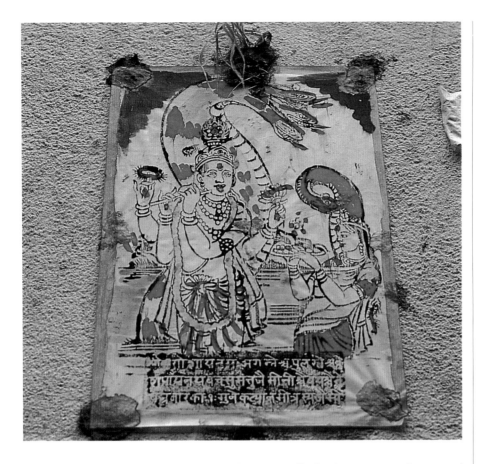

A picture of Krishna with the Serpent King behind him.

RAKSHA BANDHAN ("RAHK-shyah BAHN-dhahn") Sisters tie decorated silk threads around their brothers' right wrist and give the *tika* as signs of sisterly affection and devotion. In return, their brothers give gifts and promise to look after them all their life.

NAGA PANCHAMI ("NAH-gah PAHN-chyah-mee") Houses in Nepal are usually built from clay bricks or mud and rocks. It is common for the houses to collapse in the heavy monsoon rains. Nepalese blame this on the anger of the snake gods living in the ground beneath the house. To keep the snake gods happy, on Naga Panchami, every family fixes a picture of the Serpent King and his retainers above the home's main door. A bright red *tika* is placed on the Serpent King's forehead, the snakes are prayed to, and offerings of milk, honey, curd, and rice are placed outside.

FOOD

When two Nepalese meet on the road, the first question they will ask is *"Bhaat khanu bhaeyo?"* ("bhaht khahn-noo bhye-yoh"), meaning "have you eaten rice?" That shows how much importance Nepalese place on eating rice. Often, Nepalese use the word *khanaa* ("khahn-nah"), meaning "food," when they are talking about *bhaat*. Rice is the food of choice, but in much of the country, rice is a luxury and a sign of wealth and status.

Rice can only grow at altitudes up to about 6,000 feet and needs lots of water. Most of the country cannot meet these conditions. Rice must be carried in on someone's back in many places, raising its price so much so that many people can only eat it on special occasions.

Opposite: **A Nepalese feast fit for a king. Many Nepalese, though, never have the chance to eat such an expensive meal, and of those who do, most only eat this well on very special occasions.**

Below: **A group of Gurung women harvesting millet. Later, the millet grains will be ground to make flour, or fermented to produce liquor.**

Most people depend on other grains: wheat, corn, and millet at the lower and middle altitudes, barley and buckwheat at the higher altitudes. The grain is ground into flour by hand or water-powered mill and boiled into a thick paste or cooked into bread called *roti* ("ROH-ti").

A classic Nepalese meal is *dal bhaat tarkaari* ("dahl bhaht tahr-KAH-ree"), lentil soup, rice,

curried vegetables, which can be a very nutritious and satisfying meal. The lentils provide protein, rice is the carbohydrate, and the vegetables provide vitamins and minerals. Neither meat nor eggs is part of the daily meal. Milk and curd are more common, but still not everyday food in most houses. *Achaar* ("ah-CHAHR"), pickled vegetables, is a popular side dish.

FOOD CUSTOMS

Food is only eaten with the right hand, the clean hand. It is important to wash your hand before you eat (and necessary after!).

To eat a Nepalese meal, some of the lentil soup is poured over a portion of the rice. The soup and rice are mixed, formed it into a bite-sized portion, and popped in your mouth (all with the right hand). Then some of the vegetables, pickles, or whatever there is, is taken. *Dal bhaat tarkaari* eaten with the hand tastes better than when eaten with a fork and spoon.

All the food on a plate becomes *jutho* ("JYOO-toh"), contaminated, when even the tiniest piece of anything has been eaten. To offer it to another person is a huge insult. Any food not eaten is thrown to the animals. This taboo is not as strong with Himalayan people.

Meals are eaten twice a day, in the mid-morning and in the evening before bedtime, with a simple snack in between. Hindus are forbidden from eating any beef by their religion. Brahmins have many dietary restrictions. They should not eat chicken, duck, buffalo, onions, leeks, mushrooms, and tomatoes. All foods are classified as hot and cold based on their effect on the body. Mango is hot, yogurt is cold.

Water is usually drunk from a communal pitcher. If a person's mouth touches the pitcher, it becomes *jutho* and must be thrown out. People

To make Nepalese tea, mix equal parts of milk and water in a pot, throw in your favorite spices and bring to a boil. After boiling a few minutes, add the tea (Nepalese tea comes in loose powder form; tea bags are unknown) and boil for another minute or two. Then strain into a six-ounce glass, not a cup or mug, and drink. Sugar can be added anytime while making it. The tea should be sweet.

LIQUOR

It is illegal to make liquor in Nepal, but it would be the rare house indeed (except for high-caste Hindus) that did not. In the Middle Hills and Himalayan areas, tea and sugar may be rare, and the morning may start instead with a glass of warmed *raksi* ("RAHK-see").

There are two main types of liquor. *Chhang* ("chahng") is a fermented beer-like drink. Almost always made from rice, *chhang* is almost a meal in itself.

Raksi is the more common drink. It is a distilled drink made from any type of grain, but usually from millet. Water is added again after it has been distilled. It is usually drunk after warming it, and some butter and a few grains of roasted rice are sometimes added to give it more flavor.

Drinking is a favorite social institution. Drinks are usually accompanied by a small plate of snacks—meat, if possible. Eating and drinking are separate. The meal is not eaten until drinking is finished, which means the meal may be delayed until 10 or 11 at night. After eating, the evening is finished and everyone goes home or heads for bed.

A favorite drink in the east is *thoumba* ("TOOM-bah"). Fermented millet is placed in a pitcher, hot water is added, and the concoction is sipped through a bamboo straw. Water can be added two or three times, and one pitcher may last for hours of conversation.

Annapurna B3

Baghmati, river C4
Bardia A3
Bhaktapur C3
Bheri, river B3
Bilauri A3
Bijauri B3
Biratnagar D4
Birganj C4

Danderldhura A2
Dhangarhi A3
Dhaulagiri B3

Gorkha C3

Himalayas A2, B2, B3, C3,
   D3

Jajarkot B3
Janakpur C4
Jhawani C4
Jumta B2

Kali Gandaki, river C3
Karnali, river A3
Kathmandu C3

Keware B3
Khotang D4
Kosi, river D4

Lalitapur C3
Lumbini B4

Middle Hills A2, A3, B3,
C3, D4
Mt. Everest D3
Mugu Karnali, river B2
Mustang B2

Nepalganj A3

Phijorgdon B2
Pokhara B3
Piuthan B3

Rapti, river B3
Raskot A2
Rukumkot B3

Seti, river A2
Simikot A2

Talkot A2
Tamur, river D4
Taubhawa B4

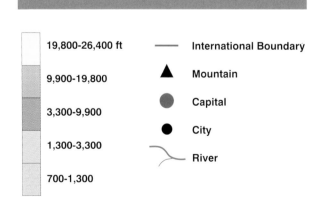

19,800-26,400 ft

9,900-19,800

3,300-9,900

1,300-3,300

700-1,300

——— International Boundary

▲ Mountain

● Capital

● City

∿ River

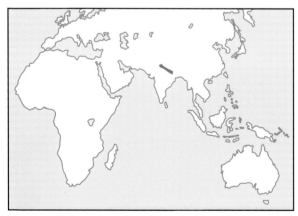

QUICK NOTES

LAND AREA
56,139 square miles

POPULATION
19.8 million

CAPITAL CITY
Kathmandu

MAJOR RIVERS
Mechi, Sapt Kosi, Tamur, Arun, Dudh Kosi, Sun Kosi, Trisuli, Marsyandi, Buri Gandaki, Kali Gandaki, Narayani, Karnali, Seti, Mahakali

MAJOR LAKES
Phewa, Rara

HIGHEST POINT
Mount Everest, also called Sagarmatha; at 29,022 feet, the highest point on Earth

CLIMATE
Varies from semi-tropical in the south to arctic in the north

RELIGIONS
Hinduism 90%, Buddhism 8%, Islam 2%

LANGUAGES
Nepali is the official language, but is the mother tongue for only about 50% of the population; about 12 other major languages are also present; English is also understood by some.

MAJOR ETHNIC GROUPS
Caste Hindus and other tribal groups, the largest being Tamangs, Gurungs, Magars, Rais, Limbus, Sherpas, Tharus, and Newars

CURRENCY
Nepalese Rupee ($1 = 50 Rupees)

MAJOR EXPORTS
Woolen carpets, jute, tea

NATIONAL FLOWER
Rhododendron

IMPORTANT HISTORICAL FIGURES
Gunakemadeva—eighth-century king, founder of Kathamandu
Jayasthiti Malla—14th-century king, made the caste system into law
Yaksha Malla—15th-century king, patron of the arts
Pritivi Narayan Shah—founder of Nepal, conquered the Kathmandu Valley in 1768
Jung Bahadur Rana—led the Rana coup in 1846, established the Rana Dynasty
B.P Koirala—led the fight for democracy, first elected prime minister in 1959
King Tribhuvan—retook power from the Ranas in 1951
King Mahendra—dissolved Parliament in 1960, re-established absolute monarchy
King Birendra—returned power to the people in 1990, currently the constitutional monarch of Nepal

GLOSSARY

bhaat ("bhaht") Cooked rice.

dal ("dahl") A thick lentil soup, served at almost every meal.

khukuri ("KU-kree") The Nepalese national knife with a characteristic curved blade.

Mahabharata ("mah-hah-BHAH-reh-tah") One of the two great Hindu epics; recounts the heroic struggle of five brothers against their five evil cousins. (See *Ramayana*)

namaste ("neh-MEHS-tay") The traditional greeting and farewell, spoken with hands clasped together.

puja ("POO-jah") Worshiping a Hindu deity.

prasad ("prah-SAHD") The blessing, usually some food and flowers received after finishing a *puja*.

Rayamana ("rah-mah-YAH-nah") The other great Hindu epic; recounts the adventures of the great hero Ram.

stupa ("STOO-pah") A traditional Buddhist structure; a hemispheric mound topped with a spire.

thangka ("TAHNG-kah") Tibetan religious paintings with Buddhist themes, usually done on small- or medium-sized paper.

tika ("TI-kah") A mark of blessing on the forehead, symbolizing the third eye of wisdom and inner knowledge, usually made with red powder.

Vedas The Hindu scriptures dating back to about 2000 B.C.

INDEX

PICTURE CREDITS
APA: 3
Liz Berryman: 71, 72, 76, 94, 102
Jon Burbank: 4, 5, 6, 8, 9, 10, 11, 12, 15, 18, 20, 21, 23, 24, 25, 28, 29, 30, 33, 34, 35, 37, 38, 39, 40, 41, 42, 43, 44, 45, 46, 47, 48, 49, 50, 51, 52, 53, 54, 55, 56, 57, 59, 60, 61, 64, 65, 67, 79, 73, 74, 80, 81, 84, 85, 86, 87, 88, 89, 90, 91, 92, 95, 96, 97, 98, 99, 100, 101, 103, 104, 105, 106, 107, 108, 109, 110, 111, 112, 113, 115, 117, 118, 119, 120, 123
Joginder Chawla: 19, 26, 78, 114
Life File Photo Library: 14, 16, 31, 62
Lawrence Lim: 36
Dr. Noazesh Ahmed: 13, 116
Dominic Sansoni: 1, 32, 82
Bernard Sonneville: 58